Marriage IS HARD

TRUTHS I WISH I HAD UNDERSTOOD BEFORE I GOT MARRIED

SUSAN BLACK

Marriage is Hard

Truths I Wish I Had Understood
Before I Got Married

by Susan Black

Cover designed by Arika Miller

ISBN 13: 978-1-936141-14-2
ISBN 10: 1-936141-14-0

PRINTED IN THE UNITED STATES OF AMERICA
BY
FOCUS PUBLISHING
Bemidji, Minnesota

For the glory of God . . .

Who has patiently and faithfully taught

my best friend Rob and me

how to love one another

and

how to experience a marriage of true intimacy and unity.

We are eternally grateful.

Preface

I cry at weddings. I'm something of a romantic. One of my favorite books is Jane Austen's *Pride and Prejudice*. Each time I read it, my heart swells with anticipation as Darcy declares his love to Elizabeth: "In vain have I struggled. It will not do. My feelings will not be repressed. You must allow me to tell you how ardently I admire and love you."

Jane Eyre is another book I love to reread from time to time. Mr. Rochester's anguished declaration of love for Jane never fails to arouse my romantic sympathies: ". . . it is as if I had a string somewhere under my left ribs, tightly and inextricably knotted to a similar string situated in the corresponding quarter of your little frame. And if that boisterous channel, and two hundred miles or so of land come broad between us, I am afraid that cord of communion will be snapt; and then I've a nervous notion I should take to bleeding inwardly." Truly, who can resist such passion?

So, I confess, I have a romantic bone or two in my body. But getting back to the point, that's not why I cry at weddings. As I sit in the congregation of loved ones gathered to witness the union of an eager groom and his radiant bride, I cry because I think of all that awaits them. I'm a romantic, but I'm also a realist, and I know that their years will contain many joys and adventures, but they will also include disappointed expectations, financial hardships, health crises, parenting challenges, and myriad unforeseen difficulties.

It's sort of like being on a highway and seeing on the other side of the grassy median a line of stalled traffic that goes on for miles and miles. As you drive past the end of the line of idling cars, you see further ahead those cars that are approaching with no knowledge of what lies ahead. Your heart goes out to them, because you know they're going to be unavoidably late. There will be frustration, anxiety, and impatience as they unexpectedly come upon the traffic jam which will keep them from arriving at their desired destination.

As I type this, it sounds to me like I have little hope for marriage, but nothing could be further from the truth. Prior to my wedding, however, no one had told me that marriage could be so tough. It was such a rude awakening—like coming upon a miles-long line of traffic when all I wanted to do was get home to a warm meal and a change into more comfortable clothes.

Early into my "wedded bliss," all of my romantic notions came crashing down around me. If I had possessed a more realistic understanding of marriage, I think I could have been a little better prepared to handle some of the disappointments I experienced when my prince turned out to be a regular man.

Twenty-nine years later, I am eternally grateful for all God has so faithfully taught my best friend and me. We couldn't have made it without Him. Romance and realism can co-exist. Love can grow deep and strong, but I believe it has a greater chance when couples enter into this commitment with their eyes wide open and their hearts attuned to God.

So when I cry at weddings, they're not tears of hopelessness and desperation, but tears of realization that the road ahead will be tough, but that love learned on that difficult road is love that will last a lifetime.

Contents

Chapter One

My Love is Not Enough

My husband Rob is a pastor, so performing weddings is one of his occupational responsibilities—one that he particularly enjoys. A couple of years ago, we attended a rehearsal dinner for a dear couple that he would be marrying the next day. We sat at a table with three young couples, two of whom Rob had married several years earlier. Because I have taught many times on the subject of marriage, I saw this as an invaluable opportunity to do a little "research" and to ask these virtual newlyweds about their early experiences in marriage. I began by asking what I thought was an easy ice-breaker type of question: "What have you experienced in the early years of your marriage that you were not expecting or were unprepared for?"

Before I relate their responses, I want to briefly describe my own experience. Rob was a full-time seminary student when we got married. I was working in the seminary library, and he was working 3rd shift at UPS. Our goal was to stay out of debt, so we wanted to work enough so that we didn't have to take out any student loans. The end result of this plan was that Rob graduated with no student debt, but we consequently saw way too little of each other during that first year of marriage.

So, when I asked my question to those young couples sitting at our table at the wedding rehearsal dinner, I was expecting them to say how challenging it was to find time together. I thought they might say that they had stopped "dating" each other and had to work at finding ways to keep the romance in their marriages. However, that wasn't at all the way they answered. One of the husbands answered first—and quickly: "She's always there."

On paper, that may look like a romantic answer, but that wasn't the tone he used. It was a mild complaint. And as he answered, the others joined in, and the floodgates opened. "Yeah, our apartment is 800 square feet, and there's no where I can go that I don't see her." Laughter. "I know. I was single for a while, and I didn't realize how hard it would be to give up my privacy." Less laughter, mounting intensity. "Exactly! I find myself just wanting some time alone, but he's always around." Lots of nods.

I expressed my surprise to them, because I was simply not expecting their answers—that they would all have the *same* response, and that they would so unguardedly express it in the presence of their spouses. I was a little sorry that I had asked the question, especially since we were supposed to be celebrating a marriage-in-the-making.

There was more discussion and then we moved on to other topics, but the conversation stayed with me for several days as I remembered some of my own distressing experiences in the early months of my marriage. During the days of our courtship, I would never have anticipated that I would be capable of such anger, unforgiveness, annoyance, and impatience. Who was this confused young bride who had had such tender hopes of a marital intimacy that would fulfill all of her romantic notions and wedded ideals?

A Veiled Warning

Several months before my marriage, I took a seminary course called "Marriage and Family Life." During that course, which covered dating, engagement, marriage, parenting, and the empty nest, my wise professor, Mr. James Hatch, read part of a letter to us from a former student who had married one of his classmates. Both of them had held leadership positions on campus and were spiritually mature and preparing for fulltime ministry. I closely identified with them—Rob and I were both in leadership positions and moving toward ministry. Like us, it sounded as if they had all the ingredients in place for a wonderful and successful marriage. However, the sentence my professor read was not what I had expected to hear. It was the husband who wrote: "Marriage is everything I feared and nothing I hoped for."

This was almost a physical blow to me. I felt so deeply the despair in this young man's admission. However, I purposely dismissed it, because I *knew* that Rob and I would *never* feel like that. People had said of us, "Oh, yours is going to be a marriage made in heaven." As I look back on the months leading up to my marriage, the statement Mr. Hatch read to our class was the only "warning" that anyone gave me that marriage could be difficult. I think that I had really believed that only bad marriages are hard, and Rob and I were going to have a good marriage.

The bottom line is that I thought that my love would be enough. I did love Rob deeply. But the thing that I didn't understand is the true nature of biblical love. What I "felt" was fiery attraction, excited anticipation of a life together, the affection born of having my emotional needs fulfilled, and a true confidence that God had brought us together. But I had no idea that my "love" would so quickly prove to be disappointingly shallow. It took me much too long to realize that it was not enough.

Disappointment and Disillusionment

I mentioned that Rob worked at UPS early in our marriage. He would have to go to bed at 8 pm, because he had to wake up at 2:30 am to get to work on time to begin loading trucks. When he got off work, he would drive to the seminary to begin his day of classes. It was a grueling schedule. We would see each other in passing when he came home as I was leaving for my job in the campus library. Soon after dinner and studying, it was bedtime.

I remember well the disappointment that Saturdays brought. My expectation had been that we would do household chores together, stroll down the grocery store aisles holding hands and chatting as we did our shopping, loll away the afternoon on our front porch swing, and gaze into each other's eyes over a romantic dinner. Rob's expectation was that he'd be able to catch up on sleep and schoolwork.

The test of my "love" during those days of disillusionment did not have an outcome that I can brag about. I failed miserably. During my lonely Saturday drives to the grocery store with my clenched hands gripping the steering wheel, I was choked with self-pity, impatience, disappointment, and anger. My love was not enough, but at this point I didn't even realize it. I was also very afraid, because my underlying belief was, as I mentioned earlier, that only bad marriages are difficult.

Love American-Style

In the early 70's, there was a television show called *Love American Style*. I remember the opening theme song, but I don't really remember much about the show. I do, however, think the title is a revealing one—there is a cultural understanding of "love" that is probably uniquely American. I believe that the American definition of "love" is one that ill-prepares young adults for the commitment and self-sacrifice that God's Word calls us to when we say "I do" to our spouses-to-be.

"Love," as depicted in current media, is rarely more than sexual attraction. While romantic love has a definite physical element, a love that lasts a lifetime cannot be based on this. It is unusual, even rare, for couples to wait until marriage to enter into a sexual relationship. It's almost expected that dating and engaged couples will live together prior to marriage. There is little in the media to suggest that there is another option; to succumb to sexual temptation is expected.

The sad result so often, however, is that distressed and disillusioned young couples discover too late that their "love" was no more than physical attraction. Love American-style leaves in its wake a multitude of broken and wounded casualties. In his book, *What Did You Expect??*, Paul David Tripp describes the moment when a bride wakes up to this reality: "Then it hits you: you married a fantasy, but you got the real person. Real people have imperfect bodies. Real people grow warts, gain weight, and get old. Marriages built on physical attraction always lead to disappointment."[1]

Infatuation is another demonstration of American-style love. It is a common and false substitute for true biblical love. Gary Thomas accurately describes the danger of building a relationship on this wobbly foundation: "Infatuation can be an intoxicating drug that temporarily covers up any number of inner weaknesses."[2]

Courtship is generally fun and exciting. We put on our best selves when we're dating, and we tend to idealize everything about our partner. The "love is blind" stage of a relationship can be blissful, but this "love" evaporates easily and quickly when hard times come or when our self-centered attitudes and actions reveal the true picture of our sinful natures. A little selfishness is all it takes to shatter infatuation.

Love American-style has at its heart an element of need-satisfaction (self-fulfillment). As long as my emotional "needs" (desires) are being met by my partner, I am content and satisfied in the relationship. When I am being wooed by my new love, I see him through the filter of an emotionally full and warm heart. My cup overflows, and all is right with the world. The problem with this need-satisfaction type of love is that it's all about me—it is self-love. I love the way he makes me feel, but my love for him may prove to be deficient and incomplete. When my partner fails in his attention to me, then my love fails as well.

"Tremendous Trifles"

During the infancy of my relationship with Rob, I was regularly looking for ways to express my feelings for him—notes in his mailbox, baked goodies that he could share with his dorm buddies, long phone conversations, enjoying time together at many of the beautiful spots around our campus. None of these things was a hardship; they were joyfully and excitedly anticipated. (I have confidence that you have experienced this yourself.) After our wedding, the responsibilities of "real life" came, and my love was tested in a way that it had not been during our courtship. If my love was blind before the wedding, then living together was eye-opening and a rude awakening.

Mr. Hatch, the professor of my Family Life class, explained a concept which he called "tremendous trifles." He explained the impatience and frustration caused by the little differences in the way husbands and wives do many things: squeezing the toothpaste tube, folding towels, placement of the toilet seat, setting the thermostat—the list could obviously go on and on, and yours and mine might be totally different. The point is that these are "trifling" issues, but the impact of them on a marriage can be "tremendous."

Mr. Hatch explained that these issues are just the tip of the iceberg. The bottom line is that they are evidence of a selfish heart: "I want things my way." Tremendous trifles expose the sin in my heart. They accentuate the fact that my love is not enough. Though they are trifling, the weight of them can crush joy, peace, patience, kindness and any other quality that should be ruling my heart and my choices.

John 12:24 says that *"unless a grain of wheat falls into the earth and dies, it remains by itself alone, but if it dies, it bears much fruit."* The truth is that I must die to self. I must realize that it is only by God's grace that I can truly love my husband in the way Scripture instructs me to love. This is so much easier said than done. It is a spiritual battle, and battles are tough.

An important step in the process is to stop putting all the responsibility of change on my spouse's shoulders. I am the only one I can change, though this can only happen by God's work in my heart. I cannot wait for my spouse to do things my way before I have a change of attitude. Mr. Hatch said that I must not focus on the partner that I *have*, but on the partner that I *am*. So I must honestly and humbly confess my own sinful responses to these tremendous trifles (calling them what they are: anger, impatience, resentment, etc.) and ask the Holy Spirit to produce His fruit in my heart (one of which is God's love).

Crackers and Crankiness

My husband Rob loves saltines. He always has. I can't really imagine that anyone has ever bought more boxes of these crackers than we have. In the early months of our marriage, he ate them with meals, after meals and in between meals. We bought a brand that used a little red metal tab to reclose the sleeve of crackers to keep them fresh.

We lived in a small duplex in which our bedroom often served as a den. Those little red tabs were everywhere. They were on the floor when I stepped out of bed in the mornings (painful), on the kitchen table, on the counters, in the bed, just about anywhere you could imagine. Those little red tabs became a deep cause of strife and conflict for me—my most difficult tremendous trifle. I could not figure out what would keep Rob from throwing them away when a trash can was so near. I built such a case against him: "He's treating me like his servant." "How can he be so thoughtless?" "Can he not see the trash can?"

I'm not sure how long this lasted. I just know how slow I was in hearing God's Spirit whisper to my heart that I was the problem. I finally got the message by God's grace and patience with me. I confessed my sin: anger, resentment, bitterness, impatience, unforgiveness. I rested in the promise of 1 John 1:9, *"If we confess our sins, He is faithful and just to forgive all our sins and to cleanse us from all unrighteousness."*

Do you understand what good news that is? God forgives us because He is faithful to the cross of Christ. Jesus died to pay the penalty for my sin, and because of that, my heart can be cleansed of ALL unrighteousness. God doesn't forgive me because I say the right words; He doesn't forgive me because I'm a pastor's wife. He forgives me because of the cross, and that will never change or fail.

The little red tabs didn't immediately vanish, but with a clean heart, I was ready to love my husband—not with the shallow love that I had brought into my marriage, but with the love of God that *"bears all things, believes all things, hopes all things, endures all things"* (1 Corinthians 13:7). In the aftermath of God's forgiveness, an idea came to me to use those little red tabs as reminders to thank God for my husband—his hard work, his desire to serve God, his commitment to me, etc. I began to do this, and then found myself looking for them!

God had truly changed my heart. It was a spiritual transformation that was not of my doing. The most interesting thing is that after a while, the red tabs disappeared. Without a word from me, for some reason Rob started throwing them away. It was a gracious confirmation from God that I had gotten His message. He was sovereign even over this small issue. In His timing, this tremendous trifle didn't depart until it had accomplished a necessary heart change in me. God had used this experience for my sanctification, and by His grace, I had taken a small step toward really loving my husband.

This tremendous trifle was a relatively insignificant problem. But the same principle applies in the more serious and complicated conflicts in our relationships with our husbands. I have arrived at the same conclusion on many occasions: God often withholds His work in the life of my husband until He has accomplished His purposes in my heart. Conflicts with my husband expose *my* sin. For real change to take place in me, I must come face to face with my sinful heart. It is then that I recognize my need for a Savior, and it is then that I can be made more like Him.

Love Agapé-Style

The truth I wish I had understood before I got married is that my love is not enough. I guess it can be said that my love wasn't really even true love—not as the Bible describes it. My love was a jumble of electrifying emotions, exciting physical attraction, stimulating compatibility, and a true desire to spend the rest of my life with the person I thought I knew and loved. However, in the early days of our marriage, my "love" was found desperately lacking.

The description of love (agapé) in 1 Corinthians 13 is well-known and oft-quoted. It was the Scripture read at our wedding:

> *Love is patient, love is kind, and is not jealous; love does not brag and is not arrogant, does not act unbecomingly; it does not seek its own, is not provoked, does not take into account a wrong suffered, does not rejoice in unrighteousness, but rejoices with the truth; bears all things, believes all things, hopes all things, endures all things. Love never fails . . .* (verses 4-8).

I must admit, I've spent a lot of time in my marriage taking into account a wrong suffered, being impatient, being provoked and unkind and seeking my own way. When those verses were read at our wedding ceremony, I never envisioned failing as often as I have. I truly believed my love for my new husband would be strong and sustained for the life of our marriage. I would never have imagined that my love was not enough.

In their book, *Peacemaking Women*, Tara Klena Barthel and Judy Dabler pointedly explain a truth that took me years to deeply understand:

> . . . Love has little to do with the object of the love. Love has everything to do with the subject **doing** the loving . . . A woman who loves her husband speaks volumes about who **she** is, not necessarily about who **he** is . . . . When a woman says of her spouse, "I don't love him anymore," it is a self-indictment, not an indictment of her husband . . . . When love in a marriage grows cold, our highest priority should be to repent, rebuild, and restore.[3]

Biblical love is hard. Marriage continually tests the nature of our love. True love is not based on my "needs" being met in the way I think they should be met. The fact is that I find out who I really am and what I'm really like when my needs are no longer being met in the way I want them to be met, or when things are not done in the way I want them to be done. I can't legitimately blame my lack of love on my husband. God's will for me is to honestly admit my lack of love and to repent. By His grace, I can move forward in rebuilding and restoring a marriage that is based on the foundation of God's true love.

[1] Paul David Tripp, *What Did You Expect??* (Wheaton, Illinois: Crossway, 2010), 175.

[2] Gary Thomas, *Sacred Marriage* (Grand Rapids, Michigan: Zondervan, 2000), 83.

[3] Tara Klena Barthel & Judy Dabler, *Peacemaking Women* (Grand Rapids, Michigan: Baker Books, 2005), 161.

Chapter Two

The Depth of My Sin

The first sin I ever remember committing was when I was probably around four or five years old. It involved stealing. One of my favorite childhood treats was Juicy Fruit chewing gum. It was so sweet, tasty and, well, juicy. My mom would buy a couple of packs each Saturday at the Piggly Wiggly grocery store when she did our weekly shopping. She was careful to limit our sugary pleasures (sugar-free gum was not available during my early years), so my beloved Juicy Fruit was a once-a-week treat. I eagerly looked forward to it (along with my weekly Sugar Daddy lollypop).

One day, my mom asked me to go to her bedroom and look in her top dresser drawer and bring her a clean handkerchief. To my utter surprise, I found not only the requested handkerchief, but also an opened pack of Juicy Fruit. I must have stared at it for a couple of minutes. It was a revelation to me that there was actually some gum in the house—it wasn't, after all, Saturday.

The temptation was too great for me. I didn't take just one piece; I took two. I reasoned that if one piece was delicious, then two sticks must be twice as wonderful. With the purloined pieces hidden in my pocket, I delivered the handkerchief to my mom. I then fled to the backyard and hid behind a tree. With trembling hands, I unwrapped the two pieces of gum and stuffed them into my mouth.

Guilt did its intended work—I couldn't even taste the gum. All of that sugary, fruity sweetness was lost in the bitterness that invaded my taste buds. I didn't understand or consider what was transpiring in my heart; I spent all of my energy getting rid of the giant wad of gum that threatened to choke me.

That was obviously not my only childhood misdeed, but during those early years, I had no understanding of the complexities of sin.

Even though I was in Sunday school and church every week, I had no concept whatsoever that I was a sinner. My unsuccessful attempt at juvenile larceny was distressing enough to keep me from choosing a "life of crime," primarily because I didn't like the guilt and anxiety which accompanied outward rebelliousness and disobedience.

I was far from a perfect child, but I was the straight-arrow type and did my best to stay out of trouble. Looking back, I now know that this wasn't because I had a virtuous desire to obey, but rather because I had such an aversion to the messiness of disobedience and the resulting weight of guilt.

In later years, when I first became aware of the concept of sin, I believed that it could be simply defined as wrong actions. I realize now how incomplete a definition that is. And I know that I can't begin to comprehend the depth of my own sin and sinfulness until I understand how the Bible defines sin and the issues related to sin.

The Sinfulness of Sin

I do not want the following paragraphs to be a dry theological discourse. The Bible is extraordinarily practical, and God's intention is for His Word to equip us to live wisely. It is vitally important for us as Christian women and wives to grasp the truths of Scripture that impact our everyday lives and relationships. Sin is not a popular topic in our culture or even in many churches. However, an understanding of sin is critical to the prospect of living a victorious Christian life and having an intimate and successful marriage. Scripture is the first place we must look to gain a clear explanation of sin and what it means to be a sinner. In other words, what is the big deal about sin? And why should a discussion of sin be included in a book about marriage?

1 John 2:16 defines sin in three categories which describe ways in which we can commit **sins of commission**: *"For all that is in the world, the lust of the flesh and the lust of the eyes and the boastful pride of life, is not from the Father, but is from the world."* Sins of commission are active sins. They include sinful actions, thoughts, words, motives, and attitudes. I may choose to eat too much (*lust of*

the flesh), covet my friend's beautiful home (*lust of the* eyes), or say hurtful things because I think of myself as better than others (*boastful pride of life*). These are all sins of commission. The list is obviously endless.

James 4:17 speaks of **sins of omission**: *"Therefore, to one who knows the right thing to do, and does not do it, to him it is sin."* This sin is a little trickier. Because I haven't actively *done* something, I may think that I haven't sinned. But if I withhold information from my husband that I should tell him (hidden credit card debt, for example), then that is sin. Withholding forgiveness, refusing to be generous, or failing to obey any of God's specific commands are examples of sins of omission.

Sin is also **inner defilement**. Romans 7:17 says, *"So now, no longer am I the one doing it, but sin which dwells in me."* Psalm 51:5 emphasizes this condition: "*Surely I was sinful at birth; sinful from the time my mother conceived me."* We are born sinners. A baby does not become a sinner the first time he expresses selfishness; he's selfish because he was born a sinner. This is often referred to as the "flesh" or the "sin nature."

Our sin is an **insurmountable debt**. Colossians 2:14 expresses this fact: *". . . having canceled out the certificate of debt consisting of decrees against us and which was hostile to us . . . ."* Psalm 38:4 reinforces the truth that we are not able to overcome the debt of our sin: *"For my iniquities are gone over my head; as a heavy burden they weigh too much for me."* There is nothing *I* can do to erase the debt of my sin.

Sin is also associated with our **inherited legal guilt** (i.e., judgment, condemnation). Romans 5:16 speaks of the tragic result of Adam's original sin: *". . . through one transgression there resulted condemnation to all men . . . ."* We may think that we are not so bad compared to others, but this verse makes it clear that condemnation is part of our inheritance from Adam. It is as if we are in a courtroom and the sentence of "guilty" has been rendered against us.

Standing as a convicted sinner before a holy and righteous judge is a formidable position. Isaiah 59:2 states that *". . . your iniquities have made a separation between you and your God . . . ."* **Feeling** guilty is not our worst problem; **being** guilty is the dreadful reality that we must personally recognize and confess. We are born sinners; we confirm it by the way we live; and we bear the condemning guilt that has plagued every generation since that fateful bite of forbidden fruit was taken so many centuries ago.

I am eternally grateful that this is not the end of the story. God's amazing grace is the subject of the two following chapters, and it is there that God's provision for our forgiveness and salvation will be discussed. But for now, we need to determine how this theological examination of sin applies to the real-life challenges we regularly encounter in our marriages.

The Challenge of Sinful Reactions

In recent years, I have come to recognize more fully the depth of my sin. This deepening understanding has greatly impacted my life and my marriage. I want us to consider a specific expression of sin to which we as women and wives may be particularly vulnerable. This is the area of our sinful **reactions** (e.g., words, deeds and attitudes).

God has created women to be relational and responsive. These are vital qualities to possess in order to ensure the warmth and depth of the marriage relationship. We are typically the nurturers in the home. We respond quickly to the needs and desires of our family members. How many times have you and your husband both been present when your child falls and cries out for help? You are often at the side of your offspring with your handy first-aid kit before your husband is even aware that there's been a mishap. We react speedily.

However, this gift from God can also present opportunities for us to be tempted in the area of reacting quickly and sinfully to the real or perceived slights and offenses that happen regularly in our busy and stressful lives. Sin can mar even those gifts of God that He intends to be blessings. Sin can transform our relational sensibilities into agitated hyper-sensitivity which influences our reactions and choices during misunderstandings or disagreements.

We spontaneously react to people and circumstances on a regular basis: jumping when startled, cooing at a baby, crying when our firstborn leaves for college. Our reactions and responses are so natural that we may think that we have no control over them. When we react sinfully toward our husbands in response to a real or perceived offense, we defend our actions or attitudes as reasonable, justifiable, natural—and even uncontrollable: "If he hadn't done that, I wouldn't have gotten so angry." "If he had been more thoughtful, I wouldn't have acted so impatiently." We imply that our sinful reactions are not our fault.

The biblical truth is that even though my reaction may be "natural" or "understandable," if Scripture calls it sinful, then I can't rightly justify it. I recently read a statement in a book that has reverberated in my heart and mind for months: "As much as we are affected by our broken world and the sins of others around us, our greatest problem is the sin that resides in our hearts."[1] When I face challenges in my marriage, it is much easier for me to say, "The biggest problem I have is my husband." However, if I want my relationship with my husband to grow and deepen in true intimacy, then I must seriously consider what's going on in *my* heart. Psalm 139:23, 24 offers invaluable instruction:

Search me, O God and know my heart;
Try me and know my anxious thoughts;
And see if there be any hurtful way in me,
And lead me in the everlasting way.

You may notice the obvious absence in these verses of any comment pointing out the sin in someone else's heart. My first priority is to search, with God's help, my own heart. Jesus points out the same truth when He talks about the log and the speck: *". . . first take the log out of your own eye, and then you will see clearly to take the speck out of your brother's eye"* (Matthew 7:5).

Please understand that I am not saying there is never any room for speaking to your spouse about a sin issue that you discern in his life. Communication is important when there are misunderstandings and disagreements. Before that interaction takes place, however, there must first be an honest and humble self-examination.

The parable of the unforgiving servant is an explicit example of this truth. In this well-known passage (Matthew 18:23-35), Jesus tells the story of a slave who is unwilling to forgive the debt of a fellow slave after he himself has been forgiven an immeasurable debt by the king. This is a striking depiction of our own unwillingness to be gracious toward our husbands, even though we have been forgiven a debt by God that we would never be able to repay (remember the **insurmountable debt** in our earlier discussion about sin).

At the cross, Jesus took on Himself the penalty for our sin, so that we might be forgiven and set free from our sin-debt. Love compels us to extend the same forgiveness and graciousness to those who sin against us. My husband should be the one to whom I'm most willing to offer forgiveness, but often the depth of sin in my own heart is the hindrance that prompts me instead to justify myself and my sinful reactions.

Our Sin Exposed

I have a childhood picture of myself holding a small paper bag and staring into the camera with a look of complete dismay on my face. I don't remember the event which prompted my consternation, but it has been recounted to me on more than one occasion.

Apparently, as a young girl, I had the habit of holding onto my belongings with a vigilance that was unmatched by my brother and sister. In this instance, the three of us had been given little bags of candy by a family friend. My brother had immediately devoured his candy, and my sister had eaten hers by the end of the next day. I had folded over the top of my bag and carried it around for several days.

Unknown to me, my dad had removed the candy while I slept one night and had substituted my carefully guarded confections with a couple of my mom's leftover homemade biscuits. The next day, with camera in hand, he asked me to show him the contents of my bag. He successfully captured my bewilderment for all posterity. You may wonder why I'm telling this story. Well, it's because this curly-haired, ponytailed girl grew up and married a man who loses things—his wallet, his keys, books, jackets, tools—you name it. Imagine that, a wife who grew up always making sure she knew where everything was, and a man who grew up not sure where anything was. God did this on purpose!

You see, one of God's intentions for marriage is to expose the depth of our sin. Let me reiterate that: God uses the conflicts in our marriages to expose the hidden sin which lies unsuspected in the secret places of our hearts. Before marriage, I didn't really know how impatient I was. Before marriage, I wasn't aware that I had such a huge capacity for frustration and annoyance. It wasn't until the "I do's" were said that I began to see the ugliness of what lurked in the dark recesses of my heart. The problem was that I didn't see it right away; I spent a lot of time blaming my husband for my sin, so that I could justify my wrong emotional responses.

The Wretchedness of Sin

During our seminary years, we rarely had any money left over at the end of the month. We made a strict budget for our meager means, and I meticulously adhered to it, guarding our few dollars as carefully as I had watched over my childhood bag of candy.

One day on his way home from school, Rob stopped to fill up our car with gas. He had taken a twenty dollar bill with him to pay for his purchase. When he arrived home, he reached into his pocket to pull out the ten dollar bill he had received in change. There was nothing there.

He frantically checked his other pockets and his wallet, but he remembered that he had stuffed the money in his pocket with his car keys when the cashier had given him his change. He realized that he must have pulled it out of his pocket with his keys when he went back to our car, and that it must have fallen to the ground without his being aware of it.

This may seem somewhat insignificant, but we really didn't have $10 to throw away. I'm not sure how to describe the emotion I felt when the reality hit me that we weren't going to find our money. It was a churning mixture of anger, frustration, fear, impatience, and pride. I was convinced that I would never have been that careless. In my heart I magnified the diligence I practiced in order to stretch our money to meet all our needs. As much as it grieves me to remember my unforgiving, haughty, and condemning attitude, I regret even more that I didn't see my own sin.

I wish that I had trusted God, knowing that His Word is true: *"I have never seen the righteous forsaken"* (Psalm 37:25). I wish that I had been gracious toward my husband ("Rob, I know that you didn't lose it on purpose—God will take care of us. Maybe someone needed it more than we do.") I wish that I had acknowledged the ultimate payment that had been made for my sin, knowing that I should humbly offer compassion to the one I loved most. I didn't do any of those things.

God arranged those circumstances to present me with an opportunity to see the depth of my sin. He wanted me to understand the wretchedness of my sinful reactions. Sin pollutes our hearts and separates us from God. It blinds us to our own depravity and magnifies in our minds the sins and mistakes of others. It elevates our self-concern and minimizes the worth of others. It whispers to us that we're not at fault and that our husbands deserve the blame that we thrust their way: *"Wretched [woman] that I am! Who will set me free from the body of this death?"* (Romans 7:24).

I feel so deeply the distressing anguish that Paul must have experienced when he wrote this. Have you ever gotten to the point in your life where you've recognized the depth of your sin? Have you fully embraced the truth that *your* sin was enough to sentence Jesus to the cross? We will never know the great intimacy in marriage that God desires to give us until we completely acknowledge that we are sinners.

A pastor friend once said, "We are not all equally bad, but we are all equally bad off." In terms of my salvation, I have as little to offer God as someone whose life has gone terribly off track. The payment required for my sin was just as great as the payment required for the most wretched of sinners.

To be able to forgive my husband, to be gracious towards him, to be patient when wronged, to communicate lovingly rather than explosively, I must believe that I am as capable of wrong-doing as he is. I have annoying idiosyncrasies; I behave in inconsiderate ways; I can be unkind, insensitive, and selfish. And most of all, I can quickly react in sinful ways when those behaviors come my way. My biggest problem is not my husband; the biggest problem is my heart.

Gary Thomas addresses the challenge of recognizing the condition of our own sinfulness: "Sometimes what is hard to take in the first years of marriage is not what we find out about our partner, but what we find out about ourselves."[2] Our marriages squeeze us. They apply pressure to our hearts. God's plan is to show us what is in our hearts—in the hidden-away places that may never yet have been plumbed.

My husband is the most important relational instrument God uses in my life to fashion me into the image of Christ. It is a slow, painful, and humbling process. It's in the marriage relationship that the stakes are the highest. It's with my husband that my truest self is revealed. It's in my home that God holds up His mirror to show me who I really am. I am squeezed, and the contents of my heart are exposed.

A tube of toothpaste can shed some light on this truth. When you squeeze a toothpaste tube, what comes out is what's in the tube.

You don't expect to see peanut butter—you can be confident that the anticipated toothpaste is what you're going to get. In the same way, when you squeeze a lemon, you get lemon juice, because that's what's inside. And when we get squeezed by the challenges in our marriages, what comes out is what's in our hearts.

The problem with this squeezing is that we don't like the person that we are when we're squeezed. We find out that we're filled with anger, impatience, bitterness, judgment, and pride. So we do everything we can to avoid or blame the person who squeezed us—our husbands. We do what it takes to keep the attention off of our sin. As long as we keep the finger pointed at our husbands, we can maintain the deceptive thinking that we're not the problem, that our anger or bitterness is understandable, reasonable and justifiable.

Jesus Speaks to a Sinful Woman

Jesus has an encounter with a sinful woman in Luke 7:36-50. He is eating dinner at the home of a Pharisee when the woman enters the Pharisee's home to approach Jesus. The Pharisee is offended and derisive. But Jesus rebukes the Pharisee, accepts the woman's worship and offers her forgiveness for her sins. He has a conversation with the Pharisee that ends with these words: *"For this reason I say to you, her sins, which are many, have been forgiven, for she loved much; but he who is forgiven little, loves little."* It is at this point that Jesus forgives the sinful woman and instructs her to go in peace.

In his commentary on the Bible, Matthew Henry explains that this verse is better rendered, "**therefore** she loved much." He continues, "It is plain that her loving much was not the **cause**, but the **effect**, of her pardon. We love God because he first loved us; he did not forgive us because we first loved him."[3]

The depth of our love for God and others is inextricably linked to the understanding we have of the depth of our sin. The sinful woman in Luke 7 was overwhelmed by her sin. She was sorrowful and penitent and approached Jesus with appropriate contrition and humility. She knew He was her only hope.

The nature of her sin is not revealed in Scripture, though there is some implication that she is a prostitute. Whatever her sin, I believe that our response to this passage should be our deep personal identification with this woman. We may not have committed the same act of sin, but our need for the forgiveness of Jesus is identical. We cannot "love much" until we recognize the depth of our sin and that we are utterly incapable of accomplishing our own forgiveness. Just like the sinful woman in Luke 7, we have no hope apart from Christ.

1 John 4:20 states, *"If someone says, 'I love God,' and hates his brother, he is a liar, for the one who does not love his brother whom he has seen, cannot love God whom he has not seen."* We must apply this verse to loving our husbands. We cannot say that we love God, if we are not actively pursuing a loving relationship with our spouses.

As the story of the sinful woman teaches us, when we grasp and acknowledge the depth of our sin and receive Christ's forgiveness based on His payment for our sin-debt, then our hearts are transformed by a new birth which issues forth in a new and supernatural love for God and others. We can *"love much,"* not because of any natural ability, but because *"the love of God has been poured out within our hearts through the Holy Spirit who was given to us"* (Romans 5:5).

Being a loving wife is a tough calling. Our love is not enough. But God is faithful. He has made His love available to us. It is to the extent that we understand and embrace the completeness of our forgiveness that we are truly able to love with the freedom and fullness that God provides to us in Christ. We move in that direction when we understand and acknowledge the depth of our sin.

[1] Timothy S. Lane and Paul David Tripp, *How People Change* (Greensboro, North Carolina: New Growth Press, 2008), 14-15.

[2] Gary Thomas, *Sacred Marriage* (Grand Rapids, Michigan: Zondervan, 2000), 93.

[3] Matthew Henry, *The Matthew Henry Commentary on the Whole Bible* (Grand Rapids, Michigan: Zondervan, 1961), 14.

Chapter Three

The Magnitude of God's Grace
Part One

I was at summer camp the week of my 13th birthday. When my friends and I boarded "THE BLUE ANGEL" (the name we had fondly given to our church bus), I had no idea that my life was about to change forever. I was excited that I would become a teenager that week at camp, but a bigger and eternally more important change was not even a blip on my radar.

During the first evening meeting where several thousand young people gathered to hear the main speaker, my friends and I were distracted by all the boys around us who were there from other parts of the country. Our young and inexperienced hearts were fluttering with the romantic possibilities of encounters with the handsome and mysterious strangers in our midst.

As the preliminary announcements were being made, we quietly pointed out to one another the boys that we were claiming for our own. As the speaker was being introduced, the auditorium became quiet, and we settled in to hear the first of several messages that were scheduled for the week.

Even now, I can't remember the exact words I heard that warm and muggy evening. I do know that I understood the Gospel for the first time in my life. Breaking through my youthful distraction, God opened my eyes and my heart and granted me the gift of salvation. It was powerful and unmistakable—I had been given new life.

I couldn't believe that I had never before understood the message of the cross of Christ. In my mind, Jesus had been just another of the characters in the Bible I had heard about my whole life: Adam was the first man, Noah built the ark, Moses parted the Red Sea, Joseph grew up in Egypt, Solomon was a wise king, and

Jesus was the one who died on the cross. I had heard that "Jesus died for our sins," but I had no idea what that meant or that it had anything to do with me personally.

On this night, however, I understood for the first time that I was a sinner. It was such an amazing revelation, because it helped me to understand what was going on in my life. I had been aware for some time that there was a troubling agitation in my heart. When I did or said wrong things, I felt terribly guilty, but I didn't know that it was "sin." I truly thought that maybe there was something wrong with me that wasn't wrong with other people.

It was a strange relief when I found out that I was a sinner. It made puzzle pieces fall into place. The best news, however, was that I found out that night that there was a solution to this problem of sin. Jesus hadn't just been someone who happened to die on a cross. He was actually the Son of God. Though He was God, He had been born a baby, lived a perfect life, and on the cross had paid the penalty for my sin, so that I could be forgiven and offered new life. It was too much—too glorious. But I knew that it was true.

During the years approaching my adolescence, I had not known what to do about the guilt that plagued me with each wrong action, word, or attitude. I had a sadly ineffective solution: my conscience seemed to grow "quieter" after enough time had passed following my wrongdoing, so I just bided my time until I "felt" better about my seemingly unavoidable infractions. However, I became weighed down with unresolved guilt. I tried to be good; I worked hard in school; I avoided trouble. But nothing alleviated the nagging suspicion that something was wrong with me.

The remainder of my week at camp that summer, I felt compelled to ask friends and strangers a question that filled my mind and heart: "Do you understand about Jesus?" I didn't know how else to verbalize the concern in my heart that there must be others who, like me, had never understood the Gospel. I wanted so much to articulate the huge relief I had experienced by being forgiven and having my sins paid for by a wonderful Savior.

Years of Frustration

The years following my conversion were ones of frustration for me. I didn't know why at the time, but I now know that it was because I didn't have any understanding that I was supposed to be growing, changing, and becoming more like Christ (the process called sanctification). I had become a Christian, but I remained an infant in Christ for several increasingly distressing years. I didn't know *how* to grow in Christ; I didn't know that I was *supposed* to grow in Christ.

At the end of my senior year in high school, I felt discouraged and somewhat hopeless. I had tried for years to do what I thought pleased God. My Christian life was mostly unsatisfying and empty. I made a decision: "If I find out in college that this is all there is to the Christian life, then I am going to have to try something else."

In His infinite mercy and grace, God provided me with a Christian roommate and Christian friends who were spiritually much further along than I was. I became part of a church that had a vital college ministry led by mature and caring men and women. For the first time since my life-changing week at camp, I was being taught how to live a victorious and fulfilling Christian life. I began to grow and change, and once again, I knew that God's way was the way for me.

Grace to Live God's Way

Each stage of life presents new challenges and times of adjustment which can be exciting, but just as often they are overwhelming and distressing. Marriage may be the most significant change that comes in a lifetime; it is all-encompassing. To endeavor to have a successful marriage apart from the grace of God is futile at best. As wives, we must understand the magnitude of God's grace; that it is richly available to us for the necessary process of growth and change that is essential in every marriage.

During my teen years, I was attempting to "build" a Christian life without any tools. It was frustrating and disheartening. You may be experiencing that type of frustration in your marriage relationship. Are you attempting to build an intimate and satisfying marriage without using the "tools" that God has provided for the job? Are you just hoping that your marriage will be durable enough to withstand the onslaughts of life? It would be a cruel and heartless god who required a high standard for marriage without providing the help that is needed to accomplish it. That is not our God; He is gracious and faithful and has provided abundant grace to enable us to be godly wives.

I have to admit that I am not shocked by current divorce statistics. I am more surprised that the rate of divorce is not higher than it is. Marriage is hard; the "job" is ongoing. But God's grace is sufficient. He is the Master Builder, and His instruments are effective for building a marriage relationship that glorifies Him.

A Definition of Grace

Grace is often defined by an acrostic: **G**od's **R**iches **A**t **C**hrist's **E**xpense. This is the wonderful grace I experienced during my week at youth camp. Jesus paid the penalty for my sin when He died on the cross as my substitute. I was offered complete forgiveness and given eternal life. My salvation was gained by God's grace alone and not by my own merit. But that was just the beginning of God's plan for His grace to be active in my life.

God's grace does more than provide my salvation. It also supplies His help for me to live in His way. I have heard grace defined as the ***power*** and the ***desire*** to do God's will. Jerry Bridges explains it this way: ". . . grace, as used in the New Testament, expresses two related and complementary meanings. First, it is God's unmerited favor to us through Christ whereby salvation and all other blessings are freely given to us. Second, it is God's divine assistance to us through the Holy Spirit."[1]

Did you realize that God's help is available to you to assist you in being a gracious, forgiving, patient, loving wife? That job description is impossible without His help. It's even hard *with* His help—that's where the growing and changing comes in. Godly wives are a work in progress.

An Earnest Appeal

Please carefully read this chapter and the next on the instruments of God's grace (i.e., the "tools" God has graciously provided to equip us to live in a way that glorifies Him). I know that you will be tempted to scan them or to skip them completely. Satan wants to prevent you from reading information that will further your relationship with God and with your husband. Ask for God's grace (His assistance) in giving you concentration for this portion of the book.

I want to stress the importance of the truth that God supplies generous and practical help, so that we can experience and enjoy spiritually healthy marriages. We cannot have a growing, intimate, and deepening relationship with our husbands apart from a growing, intimate, and deepening relationship with God. This takes deliberate thought, planning, and effort on our part.

That is why I mentioned my early Christian life at the beginning of this chapter. I had thought that the Christian life was automatic, a kind of spiritual auto-pilot. I failed miserably in my attempts to have a relationship with God. The same can be said of marriage. So much planning goes into a wedding, but it is just a one-day event. A marriage is on going and cannot exist on auto-pilot. Our relationships with God and with our husbands require our commitment and full participation. The amazing message of God's grace is that we are not alone. His grace is always available for the assistance that we need.

The Instruments of God's Grace

There are five instruments (tools) that God uses to impart His enabling grace to our lives. They will all be familiar to you, but I want you to recognize how essential they are to the health of your relationships with God and your husband. A vital relationship with God will impact your marriage in life-giving ways.

These five instruments do not represent a "to-do" list. They are the means by which God performs heart surgery on His children. They create in us new ways of relating, reacting, thinking, behaving, and believing. They humble us to recognize our need for God's involvement in our lives. They are spiritual nourishment without which we will miss out on God's best for our marriages. Please prayerfully submit your heart and mind to God as you begin this portion of the book.

God's Word as an Instrument of Grace

My husband Rob and I lived in different states the summer before we were married. My mom and I were busy planning and preparing for the wedding, and Rob was working to earn money for seminary and our new life together. There was no Facebook, email, or cell phones, so we regularly wrote letters to one another detailing our daily activities and our eager anticipation to begin our married life. It wasn't unusual for me to write two letters in a day. We both still have all those letters; his are in a notebook, and mine are in a shoebox.

I want you to imagine the following scenario: I'm being greeted by Rob on one of our weekend visits. On the table in his living room, I see my stack of letters unopened and unread. I'm understandably confused and hurt. Those letters represent my thoughts, feelings, dreams, and life-commitment. How could they be so callously tossed aside and disregarded? I return to my friend's house with a broken and bewildered heart.

This is obviously a hypothetical situation. But it is similar to how we often treat the Word of God. God has expressed to us in His Word who He is and how much He loves us. He has explained His creation of the world, the origin of sin, His faithful care for His people throughout history, His plan of salvation, and His instructions for how to live in this complex world. It is of critical importance that we spend time with Him in His Word. I wouldn't dream of setting aside

Rob's written communication to me. To do that in my relationship with God is self-defeating. I cannot fully experience His wisdom, His peace, His strength, His love if I am not partaking of this life-giving instrument of His grace.

God's Word of Grace in Action

The first time I experienced the power of God's Word in a significant way was when I was a short-term missionary in Japan (when I was still single). I was the only American living in my neighborhood. I had lived there for several months when one night I awoke to an unfamiliar noise. I drowsily raised my head but didn't hear anything, so I quickly went back to sleep. Shortly after that, I awoke again to a man leaning over my bed. In shock, I sat up and pulled the string that turned on my overhead light. I cried out, and the man ran out of my house, jumped on a motorcycle, and rode off into the darkness.

After a moment of trying to figure out what had just happened, I called the missionaries in my town to tell them about my intruder. They told me that they would come over immediately. While I paced around the kitchen, I called my Japanese neighbors who then called the police. Everyone arrived about the same time. My neighbors and friends comforted me while the police dusted for fingerprints. After the flurry of activity, everyone left. What remained with me was a consuming fear that threatened to paralyze me.

The following day, my Japanese landlord changed the broken lock on my kitchen window. My neighbors gave me a baseball bat to use for protection and told me that they would sleep downstairs in their house for several nights so that they could better hear any suspicious activity. My missionary friends came over to check on me and to offer their assistance.

I spent the rest of the week in a daze—looking over my shoulder, jumping at every noise, trying to control the tears that frequently threatened to spill over, unsuccessfully trying to sleep at night, and trying to reassure everyone (and myself) that I was fine. I had never before experienced such a debilitating fear. If you have ever had such an experience, you are probably well-acquainted with the terror that consumed me.

Now for the story of God's grace at work through His Word: Every week since I had arrived in Japan, I had attended the Japanese church in my city. The music and sermon were in Japanese, and I was slowly but surely able to understand some of what was sung and spoken.

On the Sunday after the break-in, I was scheduled to go to a bi-lingual church in a neighboring town. My fear almost prevented me from going, because the trip involved a walk to the train station, a train ride, a bus ride to another location, and then a walk to the church. I imagined every possible danger that could happen on my solo journey, and the fear was agonizing. However, I resolved to follow through with my plans and made the trip with no misfortune.

When I arrived safely at the church, I relaxed a little and looked forward to hearing a sermon in English for the first time in months. Singing the worship music in my language filled my heart and prepared me for God's message to me. The pastor began by reading the following passage from Psalm 91:

He who dwells in the shelter of the Most High
Will abide in the shadow of the Almighty.
I will say to the Lord, "My refuge and my fortress,
My God, in whom I trust!"
For it is He who delivers you from the snare of the trapper,
And from the deadly pestilence.
He will cover you with His pinions,
And under His wings you may seek refuge;
His faithfulness is a shield and bulwark.
You will not be afraid of the terror by night,
Or of the arrow that flies by day . . . .

The pastor finished reading the remainder of the Psalm, but I was so overcome by God's nearness and His tender ministry to me through His Word, that I almost couldn't concentrate on the remainder of the message. With those words of Scripture read in the language I could understand, the fear in my heart evaporated; I felt it physically leave. My tears of terror were turned to tears of gratitude and awe.

This is a long story, but the experience was monumental in my spiritual life. You see, every human attempt to alleviate my fear had failed—the new lock on my window, the baseball bat, the vigilance of my sumo-sized neighbor, the concern of my missionary friends. I was so appreciative of their care, but what God wanted to show me was the power of His Word. I understood it for the first time as an instrument of His grace.

Since that time, I have come to recognize the importance of regularly reading and meditating upon Scripture. It is God's life-giving Word to us. It's not a duty to perform, not a task to check off, not a burdensome obligation. God is a person who has graciously invited us into a relationship with Him. His plan is to use His Word in our lives as an instrument of His grace to teach us, to strengthen us, to enable us, to correct us when necessary. It is *impossible* to have a flourishing relationship with Him if we regularly neglect His Word.

This is where marriage comes back into the picture. I mentioned it earlier, and it's fitting to repeat here: We cannot have a growing, intimate, and deepening relationship with our husbands apart from a growing, intimate, and deepening relationship with God. Neither relationship can thrive on automatic pilot. God calls us to action, but it is action that is made possible by His grace.

Paul says in Acts 20:32, *"And now I commend you to God and to the* ***word of His grace****, which is able to build you up and to give you the inheritance among all those who are sanctified"* (emphasis added). We desperately need to be "built up" for the job of being a godly wife. God provides the tools for this task. The Scriptures are life-giving and heart-changing. When we experience difficult challenges in our marriages, our hearts can be drained of energy, courage, enthusiasm, and hope. We must avail ourselves of the grace ("divine assistance") of God which comes to us in the Scriptures: "the word of His grace." They provide spiritual nourishment for the relational marathon of marriage. By God's grace, this race can be finished and won for His glory.

Ask God to give you a Scripture reading plan that will work for you. It is a spiritual battle. Fatigue, distraction, and busyness are just three of the obstacles that will be roadblocks in your endeavor. Satan wants you to fail in your attempts to deepen your relationship with God and with your husband. But God makes this promise to us in James 4:6-8, *"But He gives a greater grace, Therefore it says, 'God is opposed to the proud, but gives grace to the humble.' Submit therefore to God. Resist the devil and he will flee from you. Draw near to God and He will draw near to you."* His grace is the pathway which leads to intimacy with God and with our husbands.

In the following chapter, we will look at four other instruments of God's grace. As with God's Word, they are gifts from God to equip us to meet the challenges of life and marriage and to deepen our knowledge of and nearness to Him.

[1] Jerry Bridges, *Transforming Grace* (Colorado Springs, Colorado: NavPress, 1991), 167.

Chapter Four

The Magnitude of God's Grace
Part Two

In the previous chapter we began an examination of God's instruments of grace. He mercifully uses these gracious "tools" to strengthen and equip us to become more like Christ and to live godly lives. Our marriages are an enormous and central part of our everyday lives. God's grace is the essential ingredient for an intimate and growing marriage. To attempt to achieve this type of marriage without God's grace is an exercise in frustration and futility.

The first instrument of God's grace we looked at was God's Word. Psalm 119:130a tells us that *"the unfolding of Thy word gives light . . . ."* As wives, there are countless times when we need God's Word to shed light on our dark path. If we rely on common sense or our undulating emotions to shape our decisions and influence our choices, then most of the time we will be acting unwisely. We want our marriages to deepen and grow, and for that to happen, we must be transformed in our hearts and our minds by God's Word.

Prayer as an Instrument of God's Grace

Prayer is another essential "tool" that God uses to faithfully build our lives and marriages. One of the most powerful passages of Scripture to me is the account of Jesus in the Garden of Gethsemane. His reliance upon prayer is evident as He anticipates the suffering that awaits Him. I identify so strongly with His struggle, and I'm grateful for the honesty with which Matthew relates this devastating incident during the final moments of Jesus' earthly life:

> *Then Jesus came with them to a place called Gethsemane, and said to His disciples, "Sit here, while I go over there and pray." And He took with Him Peter, and the two sons of Zebedee, and began to*

> *be grieved and distressed. Then He said to them, "My soul is deeply grieved, to the point of death; remain here and keep watch with me"* (Matthew 26:36-38).

If you have ever been tempted to think that Jesus didn't experience true suffering because He was God, let these verses pierce your heart anew as you consider the physical, emotional, mental, and spiritual torment that was awaiting Him. I've heard it explained that Jesus not only experienced temptation, but He felt it more strongly than any of us do. Jesus is the only person who ever lived who never yielded to temptation. He felt the full weight and duration of temptation in every instance—without sin.

How consistently do we bear up under profound temptation without sinning? How often during the day are we impatient, or judgmental, or unkind? We give in to temptation regularly before we have felt the entire impact of it; only Jesus has experienced the full burden of temptation on a daily basis.

This passage continues as our Savior communicates His very real distress to His Father: *"And He went a little beyond them, and fell on His face and prayed, saying, 'My Father, if it is possible, let this cup pass from me; yet not as I will, but as Thou wilt'"* (verse 39). Jesus' prayer on this occasion was no mere glib or rote recitation. He was not willing to approach the cross without the prayerful preparation that took place in the garden. There are numerous other accounts in the Gospels of Jesus going off by Himself to pray (Matthew 14:23; Mark 1:35; Luke 5:16). My thought is that if Jesus (who is God) depended on prayer, then I am being desperately unwise when I think that I can function without it. It is no wonder that I often lack the grace that I need to respond to my husband in ways that reflect the love of Christ.

In this same passage, Jesus warns the disciples about the foolishness of facing trials without the preparation that prayer offers:

> *And He came to the disciples and found them sleeping, and said to Peter, "So, you men could not keep watch*

> *with me for one hour? Keep watching and praying, that you may not enter into temptation; the spirit is willing, but the flesh is weak" (verses 40-41).*

Jesus knew that the disciples needed to be strengthened by prayer for the trial that lay before them. He knew that they were going to be tempted to abandon Him. He knew the weakness of their flesh. In Luke 18:1, Jesus had told them a parable to teach them that at all times they *"ought to pray and not to lose heart."*

Like the disciples (and every other person who has ever lived), we are prone to lose heart—our flesh is weak. Jesus knows the temptations we face as wives. We are prone to be disrespectful to our husbands, to be impatient and unkind, to hold grudges, to give the silent treatment, to keep an account of every dirty sock and wet towel we pick up. He warns us: *"Keep watching and praying that you may not enter into temptation."*

Jesus practiced what He preached. While the unprepared disciples ran for their lives, He faced His accusers willingly and then walked to His death, so that we might have the gift of an eternal and glorious salvation.

Learning to Pray

I remember as a young pastor's wife asking God to "teach me to pray." I knew that my prayer life was not what I wanted it to be. I had very little spiritual stamina when it came to my attempts to engage in regular communication with God. I was easily distracted by the demands of my busy schedule; I thought about dishes and laundry and dust. I often found myself daydreaming; I felt like I was talking to myself instead of communing with the God of the universe.

When I read biographies of missionaries and other past and present Christian leaders, it was obvious to me that prayer was such a vital and natural part of their spiritual lives. Why did it so often feel like a chore to me? I wanted to have a great desire to pray. I wanted my "prayer muscle" to be vigorous and vibrant, but instead it was flaccid and fickle.

Over the years, God has faithfully been answering my decades-old prayer. He has patiently taught me to talk to Him about everything in my life: my joys, my fears, my disappointments, my anxieties, my hopes, my failures, my heartbreaks. As He has revealed more and more of Himself to me through His Word and in all of life's circumstances, it has become my heart's desire to regularly talk to Him as the revered King of Kings and Lord of Lords and also as my dearest and most cherished friend.

In her classic book, *Stepping Heavenward*, Elizabeth Prentiss's protagonist, Katy, describes her ongoing growth in the spiritual discipline of prayer:

> I have learned, at last, to face and fight distractions instead of running away from them as I used to do. My faith in prayer and resort to it become more and more the foundation of my life. Nothing but prayer stands between my soul and the best gifts of God . . . . [1]

I am so grateful to God that He has taught me the same truth. In my early Christian life, I didn't realize that growth in prayer takes place over a period of years; it is not like instant pudding. I often find that I am impatient to be a long-distance runner before I've learned to crawl, totter, walk, and jog. But God is a patient and faithful teacher, and I can trust His time-table.

A Plan for Prayer

Prayer, as an instrument of God's grace, is a lifestyle of communion with Him. The Psalms teach us so much about prayer. In them, the various Psalmists express to God their worship, their thanks, their complaints, fears, and confessions of sin. The acrostic, **ACTS**, is a helpful tool which can provide a framework for prayer: **A** is for adoration (worship and praise), **C** is confession of sin, **T** is thanksgiving, and **S** is supplication (my requests). Over the years, the greater part of my time in prayer has shifted from my requests to my worship. I believe that naturally happens as our relationship with God deepens, and as we grow in our understanding of Who He is.

Another help for me in learning to pray has been to use regular times in the day for prayer (disciplining my heart and mind to draw near to God). When I wake up in the morning, I spend a few moments thanking God for my sleep (however much of it there was), for my family, for our home—whatever comes to mind. I ask Him to be my strength for whatever challenges I'll face. The point is to focus my attention on God even before I begin my day.

When I shower, I thank Him for my husband, and pray for him and the events of his day. In addition to a regular quiet time with God, at other times during the day (driving the car, washing dishes, folding laundry) I may give praise to God for some aspect of His character or thank Him for the beauty of the autumn leaves as I drive.

When I sin, I make it my goal to immediately confess, repent, and thank Him for the wonder of the cross that secures my forgiveness. When I go to bed at night, I often use the ***ABC*'s** to order my prayer. I choose a topic (e.g., things I'm thankful for, qualities of God's character, people in Scripture who faced trials by faith) and I draw near to God as I drift off to sleep: "Lord, I praise You as the only One Who is worthy of **A**doration; I thank you for the **B**lessing of my family; I'm so thankful for Your tender **C**are as we face the trial of cancer . . . ." I continue with D, E, and the rest of the alphabet. God's grace, through the instrument of prayer, grants peace and security to my heart and mind as I enter into sleep.

I hope this doesn't seem completely unrelated to marriage. Again, God's instruments of grace in my life (so far we've looked at Scripture and prayer) are used by God to deepen and strengthen my relationship with Him. This has a powerful impact on my marriage. It equips me in an ever-increasing way to become a wife who is able, by God's grace, to love my husband with a deeper, more intimate, and truer love than I'd ever be able to accomplish on my own.

Fellowship as an Instrument of God's Grace

Occasionally, I've taught that a husband can be a wife's best friend, but a husband can never be a wife's girlfriend. Although I've said it lightheartedly, I've been serious about the danger of expecting our husbands to bear the full load of being "everything to us." Some men may enjoy shopping, talking about recipes and diapers, and hearing every detail of our daily adventures (and misadventures). However, our girlfriends are often better equipped to "ooh" and "aah" at the appropriate times and to appreciate the challenges we face with our neighbor's unruly kids, with a stressful work environment, or the never-ending quest to think of something interesting to prepare for dinner.

A word of warning is appropriate here. The fellowship that women have with one another is important and enjoyable, but it must be aligned with the truths of Scripture. It must reflect proper love and respect for our husbands. It is so easy for a "girls' night out" to become a "let's complain about our husbands" evening. The long-term negative impact in our marriages is a high price to pay for the short-term and shallow camaraderie that results from an evening of husband-bashing. The temptation to solicit the sympathy of our friends is difficult to resist (I've experienced it), but the reward of honoring our husbands (when they're not around) is precious and priceless.

The Body of Christ

God has designed us to need each other and to benefit from our connection to other Christians. He has given us the blessing of His church to help bear the heavy load of our challenging lives—no husband or girlfriend was ever designed to wholly fulfill this need. The fellowship God provides through His church is an instrument of His grace.

As I participate in the life of my local church, God strengthens me and trains me to become more like Christ in all of my relationships, but most importantly, in my marriage. Scripture teaches me that I need the body of Christ. I cannot be the woman God intends me to be (daughter, sister, friend, neighbor, mother, co-worker, and wife) without the mutual ministry that occurs in God's church. Being a mere spectator or avoiding the church altogether will short-circuit God's purpose for His grace in my life.

In 1 Corinthians 12, Paul compares the church to a physical body, emphasizing the need that each individual part of the body has for all the other parts:

> *But now there are many members, but one body. And the eye cannot say to the hand, "I have no need of you"; or again the head to the feet, "I have no need of you"* (verses 20-21, NASB).

The truth is that we are ill-equipped and literally incomplete if we attempt to live independently from Christ's church. The body of Christ provides fellowship, encouragement, spiritual protection, provision, teaching, and a host of other benefits which God uses to equip us to be spiritually healthy women and wives. Hebrews 10:24, 25 emphasizes our need for the grace which God provides to us through fellowship with our brothers and sisters in Christ:

> *. . . and let us consider how to stimulate one another to love and good deeds, not forsaking our own assembling together, as is the habit of some, but encouraging one another, and all the more, as you see the day drawing near.*

Life is busy. Sundays are often accompanied by the temptation to stay at home in order to avoid the trials of getting our families ready to "go to church." It can be a true spiritual battle. But how often have you persevered through all the hurdles (last-minute diaper change, conflict with husband, unexpected phone call, spilled cereal) only to be deeply ministered to by the music, message, or an encouraging conversation with a friend?

That is God's grace at work—it is His plan to build us up and equip us for the challenges of our lives—including our relationships with our husbands. We need to grow and change, and God's church is one of His instruments of grace to accomplish His purposes in us.

Obedience as an Instrument of God's Grace

All throughout biblical history, God's people have proven to be rebellious and disobedient. In his decades-long leadership of the Israelites, Moses rarely had a conflict-free day. At various points along the way in their wandering through the wilderness, the Israelites were described as stubborn, rebellious, obstinate, out-of-control, grumblers, and complainers.

Sadly, we can often be mistaken for the Israelites. Their ancient description can be transported through the centuries to precisely and correctly label the behavior and attitudes lived out in our homes on a daily basis. Sin doesn't age and grow weak; it rears its insidious head in every generation.

When God calls His children to obedience, He's not doing it as a harsh and egotistical taskmaster. He knows that our obedience will open the door for His grace to be powerfully at work in us to strengthen and equip us. Scripture is crystal clear about the blessing of God that accompanies our obedience to Him:

> *Those who love Thy law have great peace, and nothing causes them to stumble* (Psalm 119:165).
>
> *But one who looks intently at the perfect law, the law of liberty, and abides by it, not having become a forgetful hearer but an effectual doer, this man shall be blessed in what he does"* (James 1:25).
>
> *Know therefore that the Lord your God, He is God, the faithful God, Who keeps His covenant and His lovingkindness to a thousandth generation with those who love Him and keep His commandments* (Deuteronomy 7:9).

God's blessing, His peace, His lovingkindness are gifts of grace that accompany our obedience. Do you remember the definition of grace that was given in Chapter 3: "the power and the desire to do God's will"? God's grace empowers us to obey Him, and then bears fruit in our lives as a result of our obedience.

Grace to Obey

I want to give a practical example of how this works in my marriage. If my husband has committed some offense toward me (real or perceived), I know that Scripture instructs me to forgive him. In the heat of the moment (anger, hurt, impatience, annoyance, frustration), I don't feel like I have the power *or* the desire to forgive my husband. I frankly would rather hold onto my anger and prove my case against him. Why? Because harboring resentment is easier than humbling myself to forgive him. At this point, I desperately need God's grace: *"I can do all things through Him who strengthens me"* (Philippians 4:13), but I truly can't do it on my own. So I pray,

> Lord, I don't feel like forgiving Rob. I'm hurt and I want him to know it. But I love you, and I want to obey you. I know Scripture calls me to forgive Rob, but I need your grace to do it. Please forgive my anger and impatience, and take your rightful place again on the throne of my heart. By your grace, please grant me the desire and the power to obey you by forgiving Rob. Fill my heart with your compassion and love, so that my interaction with Rob will achieve your purposes. Help me to remember that I, too, am a sinner, and that I don't deserve the payment you made on the cross for my sin. Help me to grant grace to Rob in the same way that you have granted grace to me. Warm my heart toward him as we solve this problem together.

This is not a magic prescription. It is the means by which I align my heart with God's, so that Rob and I can move forward in our communication to solve a disagreement or misunderstanding. It doesn't mean that we will do it perfectly, but it does pave the path that moves us toward forgiveness and restoration. It makes room in my heart for the objective truth of God's Word and the heart-changing grace that comes with obedience. It adds another layer to the strong foundation upon which I want my marriage to be built.

The Wise and the Foolish

At the end of the Sermon on the Mount, Jesus teaches a parable about a wise man and a foolish man. As you read this passage, compare the choices and experiences of the two men:

> *Therefore everyone who hears these words of mine, and acts upon them, may be compared to a wise man, who built his house upon the rock. And the rain descended, and the floods came, and the winds blew, and burst against that house; and yet it did not fall, for it had been founded upon the rock. And everyone who hears these words of mine, and does not act upon them, will be like a foolish man, who built his house upon the sand. And the rain descended and the floods came, and the winds blew, and burst against that house; and it fell, and great was its fall* (Matthew 7:24-27).

It is worth noting that the experiences of the wise man and the foolish man are almost identical: they both hear the word of God, they both build a house, and each of their houses is assaulted by rain, floods, and wind.

The first apparent difference is the foundation upon which the houses are built: the wise man built his house upon the rock, and the foolish man built his house upon the sand. However, there's another major, yet less apparent difference: those who hear the words of God and *act* upon them (obedience) are the ones who can be compared to the wise man. The foolish are those who *do not act* upon the word of God (disobedience).

Christians often wrongly assume that they will be protected from every difficult trouble and challenging trial. Looking back on the early days of my marriage, I believe that I thought we would have some sort of holy immunity to the trials that plagued other couples. I didn't think that we would have to battle the rain, floods, and wind that overwhelmed those who didn't desire to have a godly marriage.

But this passage in Matthew 7 makes it clear that our life in this world makes us vulnerable to the same struggles and challenges that are faced by everyone. Obedience to God's Word ("acting upon it") is what provides us with a firm foundation for our lives and marriages. This is one of God's instruments of grace that strengthens us to withstand the storms of life.

Trials as an Instrument of God's Grace

Scripture makes it abundantly clear that we will encounter trials and suffering as a normal part of our Christian lives:

> *Beloved, do not be surprised at the fiery ordeal among you, which comes upon you for your testing, as though some strange thing were happening to you . . .* (1 Peter 4:12).

> *For to you it has been granted for Christ's sake, not only to believe in Him, but also to suffer for His sake* (Philippians 1:29).

When trials come, we often think of them as "interruptions" or "inconveniences." But in His sovereignty, God uses trials and suffering as instruments of His grace to make us more like Christ. They are His "tools" to change us and to help us grow in our intimacy with God. Elisabeth Elliot is well-acquainted with suffering and speaks so eloquently of a lesson learned through this instrument of God's grace:

> *Eternal life means knowing God. All our life on earth is designed to facilitate that. But knowing Him must*

> *include sharing His sufferings. Instead of seeking first for escape from sufferings, the soul hungry to know Christ will seek in the suffering the means to know Him better.* [2]

If we draw near to God when we suffer, if we surrender to His purposes in our trials, if we cling to His promises when our hearts grow faint, then we will experience a new depth of intimacy with Him that would not be possible apart from our suffering. This truth is echoed by Mrs. Campbell, another of Elizabeth Prentiss's characters in *Stepping Heavenward:*

> I was bound to my God and Savior before I knew a sorrow, it is true. But it was by a chain of many links; and every link that dropped away brought me to Him till at last, having nothing left, I was shut up to Him and learned fully what I had only learned partially, how soul-satisfying He is.[3]

When God removes links from the chain that binds my heart to His, it is uncomfortable and painful. However, what I discover over time as my chain gets shorter is that I am being drawn nearer and nearer to the heart of God. I grow to know Him better and love Him more dearly. I find my soul-satisfaction in Him. This is essential.

You see, we are prone to look for our soul-satisfaction in the things of this world. Young girls dream of finding their soul-satisfaction in a handsome prince. No man can fulfill the hopes of that dream. Only God can. That is His purpose for suffering and trials in our lives—He wants to give us Himself. It is His instrument of grace to fill our hearts with what truly satisfies, so that we don't wrongly look to our husbands to perform that weighty and impossible task.

If you recognize that you have placed that burden on the shoulders of your husband, pray now for God's forgiveness and cleansing. Commit yourself anew to God and His grace. Entrust yourself to the love of God to fill the deepest needs and desires of your heart. Ask Him to help you seek the true soul-satisfaction that can be found only in Him.

God's instruments of grace (Scripture, prayer, fellowship, obedience, trials and suffering) are glorious gifts which He uses to change us, grow us up, and equip us for this challenging life. Jonah 2:8 says, *"Those who cling to worthless idols forfeit the grace that could be theirs."*

In this verse, God is warning us that if we seek to find our soul-satisfaction in anything other than Him (e.g., belongings, status, accomplishments, even our children or our husbands), then we "forfeit the grace" that He makes available to us when we actively participate with our hearts, minds and wills in the life-changing instruments of His grace. Trials and suffering may be the most difficult of these "tools." But we can trust God when He says: *"My grace is sufficient for you, for power is perfected in weakness"* (2 Corinthians 12:9a). God is faithful to use even the darkest and most difficult times in our lives for our good and His glory.

The health and well-being of your marriage depend on God's grace—only as it is active in your life are you equipped to be a wife who can truly love your husband as Scripture calls you to do. Please don't forfeit the grace that is yours in Christ. Become a joyful, active, grateful partaker of God's amazing grace. He's given you the tools—take hold of that which He has so graciously provided.

[1] Elizabeth Prentiss, *Stepping Heavenward* (Uhrichsville, Ohio: Barbour Publishing, Inc., 1998), 294.

[2] Elisabeth Elliot, *A Path Through Suffering* (Ventura, California: Regal Books, 1990), 72.

[3] Elizabeth Prentiss, p. 212.

Chapter Five

Marriage is a Process—Love is Learned

"*love* at first sight"

"falling in l*ove*"

"first *love*"

"head over heels in *love*"

"puppy *love*"

"*love* of my life"

What is love? We use the term regularly and freely, but what do we really mean when we say it or "feel" it? My first girlhood crush was Peter Noone of Herman's Hermits fame. I realize that many of you will be too young to have ever heard of this singer or his band. However, I was instantly smitten the first time I saw him on TV. I think it must have been on the Ed Sullivan show (unlike many of my friends, I hadn't fallen for one of the Beatles).

I was confused by the name of the band, because I didn't know at that time what a "hermit" was. I had heard of a hermit crab, but that seemed so unromantic, so I looked it up in the dictionary to clarify my confusion. I was shocked to read the definition: "a person who has withdrawn from society and lives a solitary existence." My dismay was twofold: Peter was so handsome and seemed cheerful and normal on TV—not at all what I thought a hermit would be like. And even more troubling, I was "in love," and if the dictionary definition was accurate, I knew that my parents would never let me marry a hermit. I was certain that except for this one unfortunate hindrance, we surely would have gotten married and lived happily ever after.

Almost two decades later, when I "fell in love" with my future husband, I was completely distracted by the overwhelming emotions of being "head over heels" in love. Rob and I were full-time seminary students at the time, and I was also a resident advisor in a dorm of about 90 undergraduate women.

Rob asked me to marry him in my final semester, and I ended up dropping a class, because my head and heart were so full of wedding planning and general in-loveness. I remember completely forgetting a required weekly meeting the resident advisors had with the Dean of Women. I had never forgotten something that important. Being "in love" for me seemed to be a slight form of insanity. I'm sure that some of my friends thought I had lost at least a portion of my mind.

As deeply "in love" as I felt, I had very little understanding of what it meant to truly love in a biblical way. I mentioned in Chapter 1 that 1 Corinthians 13 (the "love" chapter) was the Scripture that was read at our wedding. We had asked a seminary friend to give a brief message during our ceremony using this passage as his theme. Our desire was to exalt Christ and the Gospel, and I truly thought it would be a great opportunity for many in the congregation to hear a description of the true love that is available in Christ.

Sadly and ironically, I sincerely thought that Rob and I had that aspect of our relationship under control. In my mind, we already understood biblical love, and I was happy we had the opportunity to share it with others. I don't know whether to laugh or cry at how truly clueless I was. As I think back on it, I'm humbled by how patient and kind God was with us. I'm so grateful for His mercy and grace, His tender care of our fragile "love," and His years of faithfulness in teaching us to truly love.

"It's Not Wrong; It's Just Different"

Prior to my year in Japan as a short-term missionary, I attended three weeks of pre-field orientation at the mission board's headquarters.

In one of our classes, the teacher taught about the phenomenon of "culture shock." He explained the stress that occurs when someone moves from one culture to another and encounters great differences in the way things are done, the way people think, the food they eat, and the beliefs they have.

He warned us that missionaries can easily be tempted to belittle or criticize the people and customs of their new country as they encounter such dissimilarities, so he encouraged us to memorize the phrase, "It's not wrong; it's just different." He continually exhorted us to resist the temptation to disparage the very people with whom we wanted to share the love of Christ.

One of my first experiences with a culture difference in Japan was getting accustomed to removing my shoes when entering a home, school or church. On my first Sunday in Japan as I entered the little church in the city where I lived, I was rehearsing in my mind the few Japanese phrases that I had been taught, but I remembered to remove my shoes and replace them with a pair of slippers that were provided at the entrance to the building.

The unexpected trouble came when I took a bathroom break after Sunday school. No one had told me about the additional slipper change I would need to make, but I figured it out when I saw a pair of slippers by the bathroom door. On each slipper was a little toilet decal (a picture of an actual toilet) which indicated that they were to be worn instead of the house slippers that I was wearing. In my American way of thinking, I was ready to be impatient with yet another change of footwear, but I remembered my pre-field training and said to myself, "It's not wrong; it's just different."

I took off my house slippers and put on the obviously adorned toilet slippers; I was determined not to be labeled an ill-mannered American. After a moment, I heard noises which I thought meant that the worship service was getting ready to begin, so I hurried along and went back to my seat as inconspicuously as possible. As I crossed my legs, I caught a glimpse of the toilet decal on the slipper

I was wearing. Horrified, I jumped up to make the necessary slipper exchange, accompanied by the muted snickers of my new church family.

That was obviously not my only misstep in my year in Japan. But it was my introduction to the very real stress of regularly bumping up against countless cultural differences while living in a foreign land.

The Foreignness of Marriage

Marriage is a lot like living in a foreign land. Think about it. First of all, you and your husband are two very different genders. Are you familiar with the book, *Men Are from Mars, Women Are from Venus*? It was about this idea of the great differences there are between men and women—how we think, how we perceive behavior and communication, how we relate, and how we react.

If gender differences aren't enough of a challenge, husbands and wives come from two different families where there are different ways of solving conflict, handling money, celebrating holidays, and raising children. Husbands and wives generally have different temperaments: if she is a saver, he is probably a spender; if she is punctual, he is most likely late; if she is messy, he is neat. Couples may come from different generations or different countries. The point is that there are countless opportunities in the life of a marriage when husbands and wives must learn to say, "It's not wrong; it's just different."

My husband performed a marriage last year for a couple who seemed to understand this reality before they got married. In their wedding program they included a page which contained this information:

He was born in Canada	**She** was born in America
He is quiet and laid back	**She** is loud and dramatic

He likes to eat pasta and wings	**She** likes to eat sandwiches and Mexican food
He likes backhanding a ball over a short net	**She** likes spiking a ball over a tall net
He likes to watch stage performances	**She** likes to be on the stage performing
He builds computers	**She** breaks computers
He loves her energy and enthusiasm	**She** loves his patience and kindness
He proposed!!!	**She** said yes!!!

I chuckled with empathetic understanding as I read those descriptions of the laid-back groom and his dramatic bride. But I also felt so much hope for their marriage as they seemed to be entering into their commitment with their eyes wide open. I knew that those humorous differences, and others they would discover, would cause some level of challenge in the days ahead, but their love was obviously not blind; they had already encountered some of the *foreignness* of marriage and were well on their way to embracing it with good humor and forbearance.

Two Cultures Becoming One

After Rob and I became engaged, we drove to Virginia one weekend so that I could meet his sister and her family. On the way, we stopped at a little roadside truck stop. In my entire life, I had never been inside a truck stop, but Rob pulled into the parking lot like it was the most ordinary thing in the world. I was honestly a little fearful as we walked into the dining area which was filled with cigarette smoke and brawny truckers. However, it seemed safe, so I relaxed a little as we scanned the sticky menus. Rob decided on chili, and I ordered a club sandwich and fries.

This may seem odd to some of you, but I had also never eaten chili—it just wasn't a typical dish where I grew up. My mom made wonderful homemade soups, but chili had never been in her repertoire. I didn't have any problem with the fact that he ordered it, but when it came, he used the accompanying saltine crackers as his utensil of choice. He just dipped the cracker into the bowl (sort of like chips and salsa) and ate it all without the use of a spoon. It was amazing to me—and maybe mildly disturbing. I didn't say anything at the time, but I had never seen anything quite like it.

When we arrived in Virginia at the home of his sister, I was welcomed with hugs and excitement. Rob's mom was there too, and they were all so warm and gracious that my nervousness and anxious anticipation evaporated almost instantly. It was a cold winter day, and Rob's sister said that she had made one of his favorite "teenage lunches" to warm us up: tomato soup, grilled cheese sandwiches and corn chips. Apparently, Rob had routinely enjoyed coming home from high school football practice to a hot bowl of tomato soup.

Imagine my surprise when everyone began eating the soup with the corn chips. Though they were provided, no spoons were used. Ah . . . now the chili and crackers lunch made perfect sense. And guess what else! I yielded to the unintended peer pressure and ate my soup in the same way, thinking as I scooped, "It's not wrong; it's just different."

It was my first understanding that I was marrying into a new culture. Rob and I seemed so alike on our seminary campus, but here I was in his territory, and our differences were becoming more apparent. This was just one of several that cropped up that memorable weekend, and it really was a reality check for me. I had a vague subconscious inkling that *this love thing* might not be so automatic after all.

Learning to Love

Like the chili and crackers, many of the differences we encounter in our marriages are relatively insignificant and inconsequential. But when the stakes are higher (e.g., parenting, finances, difficult in-law relationships), then the prospect of truly loving our husbands becomes an overwhelming and seemingly impossible challenge.

Titus 2:3, 4 offers some valuable insight: *"Older women likewise are to be reverent in their behavior . . . teaching whatever is good, that they may train the young women to love their husbands . . . ."* There is no need for someone to be trained in what comes naturally (blinking or breathing). Loving our husbands, however, isn't an automatic behavior. We must *learn* how to love.

In the first years of our marriage, vacations were scarce. We didn't have lots of time or money to spend on "getting away." Periodically we splurged and spent the night in a nearby motel so that we could leisurely enjoy the room service and pool that provided us with a mini-vacation.

When we had our first extended vacation, it came with a certain degree of stress. Rob wanted the quietness of an afternoon of napping and reading. I was impatient to get out and explore. His preferred activity seemed like a waste of vacation to me. My desire for activity didn't seem restful or peaceful to my overworked husband.

We didn't solve this dilemma right away. We each argued the merits of our own preferences and dismissed the inclinations of the other—two "cultures" at an unnecessary impasse. We were just like the sheep in Isaiah 53:6: *"Each of us has turned to his own way."* How could the joyful anticipation of such a needed vacation so quickly turn to the stubborn defense of our own selfish interests?

In the Beginning

It wasn't long after God created man that He created *"a helper suitable for him"* (Genesis 2:18). We don't know how long it was before Adam and Eve committed the devastating sin that resulted in their expulsion from Eden, but they must have grieved deeply over all that they had lost. The first thing that Adam and Eve did after their sin was to make coverings for themselves out of fig leaves. Their next action was to attempt to hide from God when they heard Him in the garden.

These acts of self-protection were something new. Prior to their sin, they had no thought of self-preservation or fear of "being found out." Sin brought with it a tragic and sinful self-orientation that has infected every person who has ever lived.

This preoccupation with self shows up fairly quickly in a new marriage. It doesn't take long for our sinful self-interest to make an entrance. When our selfishness rubs up against the selfishness of our husbands, we behave in the same way that Adam and Eve did—we begin to cover up and hide. Walls go up, and our number-one goal becomes protecting ourselves and our own interests.

When Adam and Eve did this, it manifested itself as blame-shifting; neither of them took responsibility for their sin. On my vacation with my husband, our selfishness manifested itself when my husband and I dismissed the validity of each other's points of view on how we should best spend our time. We obviously needed God's grace—the *power* and *desire* to do His will.

Choosing Love

Love is a choice. God commands it, and He doesn't make commands that are impossible to obey. Feelings are automatic; they are usually unbidden, almost like reflexes, and feelings can't be commanded—they happen. But we always have a choice about what to do with our feelings. God is more than willing to teach us to love—to make a selfless choice for the welfare of another. His provision of grace makes it possible.

Colossians 3:14 instructs us to *". . . put on love, which is the perfect bond of unity."* This is usually easier said than done. James 4:1-2a clearly presents the predicament: *"What is the source of quarrels and conflicts among you? Is not the source your pleasures that wage war in your members? You lust and do not have; so you commit murder. And you are envious and cannot obtain; so you fight and quarrel . . . .*"

The brutal and inescapable truth is that I want my own way. I'm that wayward sheep in Isaiah 53. And if that isn't bad enough, I've also found out that my husband is one of those sheep. And now we live together. We foolishly try to cover up and hide what is so utterly and painfully obvious to our spouse.

One of the most beautiful passages in Scripture is found in Philippians 2. The apostle Paul offers us invaluable help in his interpretation of the essence of love:

> *Do nothing from selfishness or empty conceit, but with humility of mind let each of you regard one another as more important than himself; do not merely look out for your own personal interests, but also for the interests of others* (verses 3, 4).

You see, love really isn't a feeling (though a feeling often accompanies it). It is an action, a behavior. It's a setting aside of my own personal interests, and acting on behalf of the interests of another. It's regarding my husband's desires as more important than my own. Paul David Tripp says it this way: "It is self-love that makes you impatient. It is self-love that makes you want your own way. It is self-love that convinces you that your way is the right way . . . . Love prizes unity and is willing to make sacrifices to achieve it. Loves turns difference into an opportunity to experience a deeper and fuller unity. Love isn't impatient, and it does not walk away. Love perseveres."[1]

I don't know about you, but there is no way I can do that consistently and long-term except by God's grace and by the power of the Holy Spirit Who indwells me. I thank God that He delights to work in my heart to change me and transform me from the selfish person that I naturally am into a woman who is becoming conformed to the image of Christ.

Well, with God's gracious help, Rob and I did learn how to take vacations. Before we left on future trips, we began to ask each other the question: "What will make this a vacation for you?" I would express my desire (not every desire, but the most important one), and then he would do the same. The interesting thing is that when we communicated in this way, I found myself wanting to make sure that his request was fulfilled, and he did the same for me. I began to enjoy spending quiet time reading with him, without anxiously or manipulatively making sure that my wishes were granted. He enjoyed spending time in active pursuits knowing that I was looking forward to some quiet restful time back at the motel.

We continued this when we had children. It was so helpful in training them to love—to look out for each other's interests and not just their own. None of our vacations was ever completely conflict-free, but they were always contexts in which we continued, by God's grace, to learn to love.

A Lifetime to Learn

Learning to love takes an entire lifetime. Our natural pursuit is self-love, and marriage presents regular roadblocks to that pursuit. Our natural bent is to rebel against the roadblocks that stand between us and our pursuit of self-love. The great challenge in marriage is that we must learn to love the one who regularly reminds us of and exposes our own selfishness. Love that lasts a lifetime and love that is there for the hard times is only possible by the grace of God.

Dr. Harold Burchett was a professor at Columbia Graduate School of Bible and Missions when my husband and I were there as seminary students. We both benefited tremendously from his teaching and ministry. His wife Jane was a familiar presence on campus and had an active ministry of teaching, mentoring and discipling women. God used them both mightily in the lives of many students to communicate the important truths of God's grace.

Prior to his tenure at CGS, Dr. Burchett had been a pastor for many years. He returned to pastoring after several years of seminary teaching. In 1998 he left pastoring to begin another full-time ministry—caring for his beloved wife who had been diagnosed with Alzheimer's disease. In Dr. Burchett's book, *Last Light,* which chronicles the painful trials of this horrific disease, he describes the depth of love that can grow by God's grace even in the most desperate of times:

> Sometime after the neurologist pronounced over our two heads what we accept as the plan of providence for our lives, I asked Jane, "Honey, if you could have your wish, would you choose to go back like we were before the Alzheimer's, or would you rather have our relationship like it is now and have the sickness?" Without a moment's hesitation, she said, "I like it the way things are now." I agreed—and still do. We have had a good marriage that has lasted half a century, but there is a new tender caring between us now that is beyond anything we ever dreamed of in earlier years.[2]

This is God's way. He doesn't leave us as we are. The temptation is to abandon a marriage before we learn the painful lessons of true love. Gary Thomas says, ". . . I wouldn't be surprised if many marriages end in divorce largely because one or both partners are running from their own revealed weaknesses as much as they are running from something they can't tolerate in their spouse."[3] This is heartbreakingly true.

God desires to use the crucible of marriage to refine us and test our love. But we rebel when our selfishness is exposed. The refining process is more than we signed up for. We want to escape the crucible. So our response is often to resent our spouse for being the one who observes us at our worst. Even when our own sin is the problem, we make our spouse the guilty party. Fleeing seems a justifiable and reasonable choice.

To commit to a marriage can be frightening. It is fraught with unexpected and unplanned-for crises. But God's provision for this need is one of the great benefits of the cross. By His death, Jesus provided eternal salvation, but He also made available the possibility of freedom and victory in this present life. *"I came that they might have life, and might have it abundantly"* (John 10:10). He says later, *"These things I have spoken to you, that my joy may be in you, and that your joy may be made full"* (John 15:11). These promises are not just reserved for Heaven; they are for here and now.

Grace to Love

Prior to my salvation, my relationship with God could be defined by *guilt*. This was discussed in Chapter 2. I was a legally guilty defendant standing before a perfectly righteous judge. There was absolutely nothing I could do to defend myself. When Jesus hung on the cross, He took my guilt upon Himself and paid the penalty for my sin by His death. When God saved me, my relationship with Him became one defined by *grace*. All of Heaven's resources were made available to me because of this great exchange: my guilt for Christ's righteousness.

This has everything to do with marriage. I need God's grace to love my husband well. I need His grace to face up to my own sin when it is exposed in my marriage. I need His grace to stand firm in my commitment. My husband's behavior, the circumstances we're in, the trials we face—all of these things may make it harder for me to keep my commitment, but they shouldn't make me waver in my commitment. This steadfastness is accomplished by God's gracious help.

I want to share with you a poignant passage from Dr. Burchett's book, recounting the lessons he learned about love while caring for his wife in her great need:

> When I descended one night into another deep well of misery, I little expected to see something of heaven. (Around me every day, I see "free" people dancing in their dungeons of sin. I don't wish to live in such

pleasant pollution, but I admit that suffering in God's will does hurt.) At my lowest, however, I saw further up. And it was good!

A cry in the night both awakened and informed me. The worst had happened. I rushed around to Jane's side of the bed and urged her toward the bathroom, trying to minimize the trail of urine across the carpet. The balance of the discharge pooled at our feet on the bathroom floor and mat. Quite naturally at that moment, I pleaded and coerced with all my energies to get her to be seated on the stool. She stayed standing.

My energies were next directed to holding her in place while I removed the soaked nightie and protected uninvolved areas. The moment of truth for me came while I was on my knees attempting to cleanse and remove Jane from the havoc. Her blows were landing on my unprotected head. My silent outcry was, "For this I get that?!"

Right then heaven suddenly opened over my deep well. I could see and hear—not with eyes and ears, but with heart—the Lord Jesus saying, "Now you know some of what I suffered for, and from, you. And what you did, you did with healthy brains!" It is clearer now that "God demonstrates his own love for us in this: While we were sinners, Christ died for us" (Romans 5:8). Jesus' death was indeed for "God's enemies" (verse 10).

The same insight was underscored for me one morning while I was still serving as senior pastor. My secretary interrupted my studies to tell me that the volunteer caregiver at home was calling because of an emergency. Jane was refusing to finish dressing, so they could not go out to lunch as planned. "Get her topcoat on, and bring her to me," I suggested.

> The plan fell apart at the church door. Slipping off the covering cloak, Jane strode into the hallway of the office wing dressed as she was at home: little nightie with two skirts and a pair of slacks underneath. I stepped from my office at the opposite end of the passage. What a pitiful sight she was, standing there at the far end of the hall, alone, unprotected, exposed! All the church's administrative and pastoral offices open on that busy hallway. It seemed a mile long as I rushed to meet her.
>
> Being so intent on gathering Jane into my arms and shielding her from view, I was not conscious of those around. I drew her directly into my office. There in safety and seclusion, I held her until she understood that all was well.
>
> My understanding also opened. I saw it clearly. The Lord Jesus had rushed to my aid and, bearing my shame and sin, He now shields me from all accusation. He shows more love to his Bride than I could ever show to mine (Used by permission).[4]

Here's the amazing thing. When I choose to love my husband by God's grace and the power of the Holy Spirit who indwells me, then not only am I empowered to love my husband well, but it also enlarges my heart to know God more deeply and to love Him more fully. It deepens my understanding of my need for God, and it increases my gratefulness for His amazing grace.

This is not an ordinary or natural event. A genuine spiritual transformation is taking place in my heart. There is an increasing capacity for love that wasn't there before. And over the years, as I continue to choose to love by God's grace, then that true biblical love becomes more and more a part of my character—the old ways are truly being left behind—new ways have come (2 Corinthians 5:17). In my marriage, that translates into deeper commitment, greater friendship, truer intimacy, and a more profound devotion. In my relationship with God, it translates into utter soul-satisfaction as I come to know first-hand His intimately personal provision and faithfulness.

God's ways are mysterious and often difficult, but they are better than life. His grace is sufficient for every trial and challenge that you encounter in your relationship with your spouse. Marriage is a process; true love has to be learned. God is your faithful and gracious teacher; marriage is your classroom.

[1] Paul David Tripp, *What Did You Expect??,* 171.

[2] Harold Burchett, *Last Light* (Colorado Springs, Colorado: NavPress, 2002), 12-13.

[3] Gary Thomas, *Sacred Marriage,* 97.

[4] Burchett, 119-120.

Chapter Six

Expectations Can Be Deadly

Christmas had come and gone when my parents offered me the "big-girl" privilege of staying up with them to welcome the New Year. Unless it snowed, this was the best opportunity for excitement before heading back to school from our Christmas break. I was still a young girl and had never been allowed to stay up this late. I tried to calmly receive the invitation; I didn't want to do anything to make them rethink their offer. Still holding my breath, I ran back to my room to tell my older sister that my turn had come.

I counted down the days until New Year's Eve finally arrived. I was so excited that I could hardly eat my dinner. As the midnight hour approached, I sat between my mom and dad on the couch watching the event on television. I wondered if they could feel the vibration of my throbbing heart. Before I knew it, they were waking me up to let me know that it was almost midnight. I couldn't believe that I had fallen asleep—I had almost missed the big moment.

We started counting the seconds down, and I ran to the window to "watch" the New Year arrive. When we got to zero . . . nothing happened. It was dark outside, so I couldn't see much, but I could tell that nothing had changed. I don't know what I had expected to see, but I knew I was supposed to be "watching" the New Year come in, and in stunned bewilderment I realized there was nothing to observe. My "big-girl" moment was a monumental let-down.

Everyone has expectations. According to the dictionary, when we *expect* something to happen, then we look forward to its "probable occurrence or appearance." One synonym of expect is hope, which means to "desire, usually with confidence in the likelihood of gaining what is desired." Even the definition carries with it the prospect of great frustration. If we are confident that we are going to get what we desire, then there is a great possibility that the outcome of our unmet expectation will be disappointment. Added to that, we usually have much greater expectations of those we love the most. After all, doesn't love mean that the ones who love us desire to make us happy and fulfill all our wishes?

So, what do I mean by the title of this chapter: that "expectations can be deadly"? That sounds a bit dramatic. One of the dictionary definitions of *deadly* is "destructive in effect." In this sense, expectations in a marriage can often be *deadly.* The casualty can be the marriage itself, but the lethal effects of expectations can also extend to the inner workings of our hearts—effects that we may not completely recognize and understand until the deadly damage has been done. The wounds of unmet expectations often fester into disillusionment, disrespect, anger, and bitterness. How can we understand this occurrence and ensure that we guard against the destructive impact of unmet expectations in our marriages?

Early Expectations

In the family in which I grew up, being prompt was a big deal. It was considered an important courtesy, and it was taken for granted that we would extend that respect to others. It was so much a part of my life that I didn't really give it much thought as I grew older; being on time was just as routine as brushing my teeth or putting on a seatbelt.

And now . . . the plot thickens. I spent the first decades of my life as a worrier: "Hello. My name is Susan, and I am a fretter." I worried about everything—it was like a reflex. I grew up believing that my worry, anxiety, and fretfulness were simply evidence that I cared deeply about whomever or whatever happened to be the source of my concern. I never spiritually understood the havoc that anxiety was wreaking in my life.

My husband Rob is the youngest of three. When he was in high school, his older brother and sister had moved on to college and beyond. He had his own car and came and went according to his work and football schedule. There was no real curfew to keep, so there was never a set time when he was expected to be home. And his parents were not the anxious types (I didn't know there was such a thing as people who weren't plagued by worry).

As Rob and I were moving toward engagement, he went home one weekend to visit his dad who was critically ill with colon cancer. He had told me that he'd probably get back to campus on Sunday evening around 5:00 pm. You might guess where this is going. By 5:05 I was an absolute wreck. There were no cell phones then, so there was no way to contact him. Fear gripped my heart, and I honestly had the thought that I should go to the dining hall to eat supper, so that I would be strong when the authorities came to tell me about Rob's car accident. Crazy!

A couple of hours later he casually called to tell me that he was back on campus. My relief exploded into tears and sobs, and Rob was understandably perplexed by my emotional outburst. On this occasion, I didn't experience anger or resentment, because I was so relieved that he was safe. And for him, his late return to campus was no big deal—in his home he had never really had to contend with a fretful mom or a concrete arrival time.

However, when this experience was repeated in our marriage, I began to attach to it *my* interpretation of his motives and behavior: rudeness, selfishness, and disregard for my feelings. It didn't occur to me to take into account his background or that patient communication and thoughtful understanding could assist us in learning how to live together.

In *Peacemaking Women*, Tara Klena Barthel and Judy Dabler include an invaluable and insightful explanation of something they call "the expectation-experience gap":

> While some expectations are legitimate, many of our expectations are unrealistic because they require far more than anyone can give. We look for people to say, do, or be something specific—and then they fail to

> meet our expectations. We encounter a "gap" between what we hope for and what we actually experience.[1]

Although we may not be aware of it, we all experience the reality of this gap. I fell face-forward into the gap when I began to fuss, fume and fret because of my husband's habitual tardiness. The even bigger problem came when I assigned motives and intentions to his actions. Rob was not being maliciously late or thoughtlessly tardy. Being prompt had not been the virtue in his family that it had been in mine. There was a considerable gap in our understanding of each other and in our communication with each other. We needed help.

The expectation-experience gap does not have to be a threatening and unavoidable abyss. By God's grace we can choose to fill the gap with those things which bring intimacy and depth to our relationships with our husbands. We must first, however, understand our expectations and the influence and power they can wield in our marriages.

The Origin of Expectations

We bring conscious and subconscious expectations into our marriages. They may be as simple as a desire for a clutter-free house or flowers on special occasions. They may also be more complex, as in determining what role each spouse will have in the relationship or where and how to celebrate holidays. So many factors go into determining what expectations we have, but fallout as a result of unmet expectations is universal.

Our personal expectations find their origin in our thinking. Our thinking is influenced by a host of different factors. I've already given an example of how my family background produced in me an expectation of punctuality. There is not space or time to do an exhaustive study on all the sources of our expectations, but one that is particularly relevant is the portrayal of romantic relationships in current media.

Romantic comedies and dramas are frequently labeled "chick flicks." Women are drawn to movies that stir their hearts. I mentioned in Chapter 1 that God has created women to be relational, and that's a good thing. However, it can lead us down a difficult road. It's exciting and titillating to follow the twists and turns of a "boy meets girl" plot as it's building to the desired conclusion of requited love and blissful marriage. The problem comes when I expect my husband to deliver to me on a daily basis that degree of heart-throbbing emotion.

If expectations begin in my thinking, then I must become insightfully aware and vigilantly attentive to how my thinking is influenced. Am I going to allow my background or the media to shape my thinking, or am I going to make sure that the truths of Scripture inform and transform my mind? Romans 12:1-3 gives clear instruction about this:

> *I urge you, therefore, [sisters], by the mercies of God, to present your bodies a living and holy sacrifice, acceptable to God, which is your spiritual service of worship. And do not be conformed to this world, but be transformed by the renewing of your mind, that you may prove what the will of God is, that which is good and acceptable and perfect. For through the grace given to me I say to every [woman] among you not to think more highly of [herself] than [she] ought to think; but to think so as to have sound judgment, as God has allotted to each a measure of faith.*

Our minds must be renewed by the truths of Scripture and by the work of the Holy Spirit. My expectations may be legitimate and justifiable—*if* they are aligned with God's truth. By His grace, I can learn to recognize the expectations that I have, evaluate them by God's Word, and be willing to set them aside when they have been born by wrong thinking.

Please regard soberly the role of God's grace in this process; only God can change our faulty thinking; only He can renew our minds. He uses His Word and the ministry of the Holy Spirit to accomplish this. Remember to actively participate in the process by engaging in the instruments of God's grace that we discussed in Chapters 3 and 4. God can grant to us sound judgment and humility, so that we can offer patience and grace to our husbands when our hopeful expectations are unfulfilled.

The Idolatry of Expectations

My first understanding of idols came from my Sunday school days when we read in Exodus about the golden calf that Aaron made when Moses was on the mountain receiving the Ten Commandments from God. When Aaron presented the calf to the Israelites, they said: *"This is your god, O Israel, who brought you up from the land of Egypt"* (Exodus 32:4). There was absolutely no mistaking the fact that the molten calf was an idol.

Present-day idols may be more difficult to recognize, but it is crucial for us to be able to identify the idols in our own hearts. The first of God's commandments to His people was: *"You shall have no other gods before Me"* (Exodus 20:3). It is clear that this is of uppermost importance to God, so it must carry that same weight for us.

When I think of the idols in my life, I picture my heart inhabited by a throne. There should be nothing or no one on that throne but Christ alone. Anything else on that throne is a substitute for God: anything or anyone I love, serve, desire, or worship in place of God.

I may look to food to give me comfort instead of looking to the comfort offered graciously and fully by God. I may think that my health or finances can provide security for my family instead of recognizing that God is the source of all my security. I may value my friendships above the relationship that I have with God. And when my expectations rule my thinking, emotions, responses, and mood, then I have given them idol status in my heart.

"*. . . Some form of idolatry exists at the root of every human conflict.*" [2] That is true regarding my conflicts with my husband. I can know that my expectation is an idol by the way I respond to my husband when my expectation is not met. When my idol is being threatened or exposed, I lash out at the one whom I perceive as the threat. My sinful reactions may take many forms: withdrawal, verbal attack, silent treatment, manipulation, judgment, resentment, pouting. What those reactions reveal is the idolatrous golden calf hunkered down on the throne of my heart.

Our idols can rear their ugly heads over the simplest infractions. If our husbands leave a wet towel on the floor, or if they unexpectedly work late, or if they forget an anniversary, then there is a good chance that we will make sure that they are fully aware of our displeasure. What usually happens is that we replay the offense over and over in our minds, justifying our own sinful responses while building an air-tight case against our husbands. When they arrive on the scene, the judgment has been made and the sentence is ready to be delivered. Psalm 115 describes idols and those who make them:

> *Their idols are silver and gold,*
> *The work of man's hands.*
> *They have mouths, but they cannot speak;*
> *They have eyes, but they cannot see;*
> *They have ears, but they cannot hear;*
> *They have noses, but they cannot smell;*
> *They have hands, but they cannot feel;*
> *They have feet, but they cannot walk;*
> *They cannot make a sound with their throat.*
> ***Those who make them will become like them,***
> *Everyone who trusts in them* (verses 4-8, emphasis mine).

Verse 8 of this passage has always intrigued me. I believe it means that as I give honor to the idols of my heart, I become increasingly more self-concerned and less and less concerned for others. I grow insensitive (i.e., cannot speak, see, hear, smell, feel, walk, make a sound) to the needs of my husband. Furthermore, I tend to misinterpret the meaning of his words, and I don't see the true or full picture of the conflict we may be in. In short, I am becoming like my idol. As long as I am protecting and clinging to my idolatrous expectation, I will never be able to relate to my husband in a way that honors God.

Choosing God's Way

When there is a gap between what I expect and what I actually experience, then I must recognize that I am responsible to fill the gap in a godly way. When I put all of my emotion and energy into the disappointment or frustration I experience when my expectations are not met, then I will certainly fill the gap with self-pity or nagging or criticism. I cannot control whether or not my husband will fulfill all my desires, but I can, by God's grace, choose to fill the gap with what honors Him: patience, kindness, honest and loving communication, confession, and repentance.

If I choose to live by my feelings, then I will fill the gap with what brings me temporary "relief" or the attention that I desire: venting my anger, accusing my husband, expressing my annoyance. However, if I choose to live by God's truth and its transforming power in my heart and mind, then I will fill the gap in a way that brings glory to God.

Scripture is replete with instruction: be kind to one another; treat others as you want to be treated; consider others as more important than yourself; die to self; do not judge; put away anger and bitterness. I cannot do any of this on my own; I am not naturally prone to live in a selfless way. My idols are powerful; they do not want to surrender their occupation of my heart's throne.

Choosing to live God's way is a spiritual battle. When I engage in this battle, this is an example of the way I pray for God's help:

> "Father, there is a battle raging in my heart. I confess
> to you that I have replaced Christ on the throne of my

> heart with the idol of desiring my own way. I am not being ruled by your love, but by my own selfishness. I confess my anger and impatience and lack of love. You promise in your Word that if I confess my sin, you are faithful and righteous to forgive my sin and to cleanse me from all unrighteousness. I thank you for your forgiveness that came at the cost of Christ's death on the cross. I praise Him as Lord and ask that He would rule again on the throne of my heart. Scripture also says that if I resist Satan, he will flee from me. So, in Jesus' name, I resist him and ask for your protection as Rob and I work together to solve this conflict. I ask that the Holy Spirit would fill my heart with His love, peace, patience and kindness. And I thank you for your grace that enables us to choose your way and to move toward forgiveness and restoration. Please help us now in Christ's name, Amen.

God gives grace to choose, grace to pray, and grace to solve conflict. The idol of my expectations cannot conquer the God of all creation.

Marriage with a Purpose

God's purpose for marriage in our lives is not simply to make us happy. To think that our marriages are all about us is short-sighted and self-centered. God desires to use our marriages as a context in which He changes us and makes us more like Christ. Our expectations are used by Him to reveal to us the idolatry in our hearts. God's gracious plan is to replace our deadly expectations with a life-giving and self-sacrificing love that leads to a true fulfillment which can be found only in Him.

You may be wondering if I'll ever get back to the punctuality expectation that I described at the beginning of this chapter. Well, God used Rob's tardiness to teach me patience and self-control. I *really* needed a lot of practice to learn how to exhibit those fruits of the

Spirit in my life. God knew that Rob's tendency to be late was exactly the circumstance I needed to reveal to me my sin of impatience and quickness to judge. (Remember from Chapter 2, the biggest problem I have is the sin in my own heart.)

Once again, as I became more sensitive to the Spirit's prompting, more attuned to God's instruction in Scripture, and more obedient in my attitudes and actions, then He transformed my thinking and helped me to change. And over the years, Rob has become consistently prompt. In this particular instance, he simply needed a change of habit. My need was greater: I needed a change of heart.

I also realized that I had assigned to Rob the responsibility of making me feel safe. If he was late, then my security was threatened. That was an idolatrous expectation. I began to understand that my security had to be in God and God alone—regardless of my circumstances. I am so grateful to God that He was faithful to topple that destructive and entrenched idol.

Expectations can be deadly. They can smother the life and joy out of a marriage. I cannot place the weight of all my expectations on the shoulders of my husband. I cannot look to him to fulfill all of my hopes. John Ensor says it so well: "Sisters, to look to any man to be your all-consuming delight is to set him up for failure, and then you will hate him for disappointing you. You will find what you are seeking only in Christ."[3]

[1] Tara Klena Barthel & Judy Dabler, *Peacemaking Women* (Grand Rapids, Michigan: Baker Books, 2005), 149.

[2] Ibid, 47.

[3] John Ensor, *Doing Things Right in Matters of the Heart* (Wheaton, Illinois: Crossway Books, 2007), 49.

Chapter Break

Sixth Inning (Chapter) Stretch

In baseball, a break called the "Seventh Inning Stretch" occurs halfway through the seventh inning. It's a short break intended to give the players a brief respite and to give the fans an opportunity to stand and stretch and perhaps get something to eat or drink.

I'm not really a big baseball fan, but as I've been writing, I've had a growing realization that I want to take a bit of a break to properly introduce you to my husband. He has, after all, been a main character in this book, and I want to give him my great thanks for his willingness to have our marriage become "an open book" (no pun intended). He loves sports, so he'll be (mildly) impressed that I've found a way to include a sports reference in his honor.

I'm doing a *sixth* chapter stretch, because I haven't yet written chapter 7. And I want to do it today, because as I'm typing this very page, Rob and I are celebrating our 28th anniversary. He's been giving me periodic kisses which should add up to 28 by the time our heads hit our pillows tonight. We've both been so grateful today for God's faithfulness to us over the years. He's taught us to love one another, and His grace has carried us through every trial we have encountered.

Rob loves to read and fish. He loves *The Andy Griffith Show*, and he is a die-hard University of Kentucky Wildcats fan (we spent 10 years in Georgetown, Kentucky). He is a gifted counselor, teacher, and discipler. He's been the Pastor of Adult Ministries at our church for 11 years. He's currently writing his doctoral thesis, so a lot of typing has been going on in our home this year. He is also an amazing father. Our three sons are grown (our oldest son, Andy, is married to our beautiful and creative daughter-in-law, Kara, and our younger two, Thomas and Philip, are in college).

About 6 months ago, Rob was diagnosed with a rare cancer; an ocular melanoma. These past months have been filled with doctor's appointments, surgeries, examinations, and other treatments. We have had some dark and fearful moments, but God has been faithful to fill our hearts with peace and confidence in His sovereignty.

Rob's cancer has been a gift to us in many ways, but one of the main ways has been the deeper closeness that we have experienced in our marriage. I believe I can truly say that we have more contentment on this anniversary than we have ever yet experienced.

I feel compelled to share this, because I don't want you to think that I'm writing this book from some theoretical or academic perspective. I believe that one of God's purposes in all that Rob and I have learned in our marriage has been to prepare us for this new chapter in our lives.

Prior to Rob's diagnosis, we had thought that we might have a bit of a let-up in our lives. We had recently emptied our nest when our youngest son had gone off to college. Our church had hired a new senior pastor, so Rob's duties were going to return to the normal busy rather than the frenetic busy that had been his life for such a long time. We were looking forward to "dating" again—just the two of us.

But God had other plans—better plans. And although we were already best friends, God has given us a greater and deeper intimacy—a further pruning of our relationship with the blessed promise of more beautiful fruit.

So as I write this, I want to encourage you to think of your marriage from God's point of view. He knows what's coming in your life, and you are going to want to have a companion, a best friend, a true partner to share the good times and to walk with you in the dark times. It is often so easy to think that it's us vs. our husbands. But God's plan is to use the difficulties we face to show us who He is and who we are. He is about the business of changing us and maturing us for His good purposes.

Marriage is hard. But the battle for your marriage is worth it. Take seriously the challenge to be growing in the grace of God. Remember that it's not about you. God's plan is so much bigger, and His desire is to use all of the trials you face to push you towards Him. You will find Him faithful for every need you have.

And now it's time to get back to the game (Chapter 7).

Chapter Seven

Respect is Given, Not Earned

". . . and let the wife see to it that she respect her husband" (Ephesians 5:33b). These words often strike fear into the hearts of women. I know that when I was a young girl, my mom would introduce her instructions in a similar way: "See to it that you eat all of your vegetables." "See to it that you clean your room before dinner." "See to it" meant that I should make sure that it happened. My mom's words weren't a suggestion, but a definite command.

Paul's instruction to wives carries the same weight. He is not saying that respecting our husbands is a clever concept or an amusing pastime—he's saying, *"Do it."* In the same way that love is primarily an act of the will, respect for our husbands is primarily an action or an attitude. Feelings often accompany acts of love and respect, but our choice to perform these actions should not depend on our feelings. They are acts of obedience to God.

Respect does not come naturally. Eve's sin in the Garden of Eden was laden with disrespect—toward God and Adam. God was not ambiguous in His communication to Adam and Eve that the tree of the knowledge of good and evil was off-limits to them (Genesis 2:17). Eve, however, decided to do her own thing in her own way. Perhaps if she had first spoken to God or to her husband she would have been more perceptive in recognizing the deception of Satan.

Respect for husbands has been a source of struggle for women since that woeful day. So Paul's instruction is a crucial and necessary reminder. We need to be told, because we don't instinctively behave in this way. In his first epistle, the apostle Peter confirms the truth that respect is primarily an action. He says in chapter 3 that disobedient husbands may be won *"as they observe your chaste and respectful behavior"* (verse 2). Again, he's not speaking of a feeling. Carolyn Mahaney says,

> So even if we do not feel particularly respectful today, or though we may not think our husbands have done anything worthy of respect lately, or even if we reckon ourselves to be more capable, intelligent, or godly than our husbands—none of these reasons exempt us. Respect is a decision we make to obey God's Word.[1]

I want to encourage you to give the same consideration to your husband that you would, no doubt, give to a friend. Do you drop what you're doing to go to her aid? Do you speak with consideration and circumspection to avoid unnecessarily hurting her feelings? Do you regard her likes and dislikes when making a decision? Do you show enthusiasm and interest when she's telling you about an experience she has had? Do you offer her your support and love when she is discouraged?

Respecting your husband is a Golden Rule sort of behavior. This guiding principle does not say to treat others the way that you're treated, but rather to treat others in the way you *want* to be treated (Luke 6:31). Romans 12:10 tells us to *"give preference to one another in honor."* The side note in my Bible says to *"outdo one another in showing honor."* How often does that happen in our marriages? Do we consciously attempt to show more honor to our husbands than they show to us? This is a tall order, but a worthy one, and one that is possible by the grace of God.

The Missing Piece of the Puzzle

Have you ever finished putting together a large puzzle only to find that the final piece is missing? There is usually a valiant effort expended to locate that missing piece. Our family has been on that vain search many times: couch cushions tossed, blankets shaken, boys' pockets checked (more than one of our sons has used this method to ensure that he'd be able to put in the last piece), and dog bed scoured—usually to no avail.

I want you to picture with me your husband as a giant jigsaw puzzle. All the pieces are in place with the exception of one. In this picture, you are standing beside him holding up that valuable missing piece. As long as it remains in your grip, the puzzle won't be complete. There's a caption above your head that expresses the attitude of your heart, "I'll give you your missing piece . . . as soon as you start behaving like a real man."

I hope the irony is obvious. As wives, we often withhold respect from our husbands until we feel that they have earned it. The problem often is, however, that they won't be equipped to be the men we want them to be until we supply the missing piece of the puzzle: respect. As long as we refuse to make it available, we're in a no-win situation. Our husbands will never be the men we want them to be, and we'll hold ever more tightly onto the respect that they desire so deeply.

Our respect helps to equip our husbands for the demands in their lives. Their desire for our respect is not a sin. We shame our husbands when we have disdain for them or belittle them because of their desire for our respect. Proverbs 12:4 says, *"An excellent wife is the crown of her husband, but she who shames him is as rottenness in his bones."* To shame our husbands is a desperate tragedy. Our disrespect drains our husbands of vitality, confidence, and hope. They need all three in great measure to withstand the challenges, battles, and temptations of their day-to-day lives. You hold that indispensible piece of the puzzle. What will you do with it?

Enemies of Respect

One of the greatest enemies of respect is comparing our husbands to others: "the grass is always greener on the other side." We can convince ourselves that if our husband was like Betty's husband, then he'd be easy to respect. We can dream of a movie star husband who knows just the right thing to say, wear, and do (those husbands surely never walk around in their tattered underwear, belch in appreciation of their delicious supper, or make an embarrassing faux-pas in a social situation).

As wives, we must accept responsibility for respecting our husbands. Our disrespect cannot be blamed on whether or not our husbands' performance meets up to our particular standard. If we do not respect the man we married, we must acknowledge and confess that we wouldn't respect any other husband. Respect is a choice I make by the grace of God. It isn't dependent on my spouse. Gary Thomas echoes this sobering reality:

> Wives, you are married to a sinful man in a sinful world. It is guaranteed that your spouse will sin against you, disappoint you, and have physical limitations that will frustrate and sadden you. He may come home with the best of intentions and still lose his temper . . . . You will never find a spouse who is not affected in some way by the reality of the Fall. If you can't respect this spouse because [he] is prone to certain weaknesses, you will never be able to respect any spouse.[2]

I have a godly friend, now a widow, who had been married for decades to her non-Christian husband. One Sunday morning I was sitting beside her in a class my husband was teaching. After a particularly meaningful lesson, she said, "Oh, what must it be like to be married to such a man?" With a chuckle and a raising of my eyebrows, I replied, "How much time do you have?"

You see, I am married to a wonderful man, but I know the reality of living with another sinner. In my friend's mind, she really believed what she wistfully expressed in her question: *what bliss it must be to live with a godly man*. I don't take for granted how blessed I am to live with a man who is committed to God and to me, but those treasured qualities don't immunize me against encountering the same challenges in marriage that everyone else experiences. To be respectful toward my husband is a choice, but it's one that I cannot make consistently except by the grace of God.

An important principle that I've previously discussed must be repeated here: God's plan is to keep us, His children, in the process of growing and changing (sanctification). It's a life-long and costly step-by-step transformation. He knows that we can't accomplish it on our own, so He surrounds us with people and circumstances which put the squeeze on us.

When that squeezing happens, our fleshly reflex is to blame and find fault with the person involved in God's squeezing process: "There he goes again! How can I respect a man who acts like that? If he would just grow up and change, I wouldn't have any problem respecting him!"

This is where marriages get stuck. The soaring divorce rate is evidence of it. Men and women believe that a change of spouses will solve the problem. But they take their sinful hearts into a new marriage, and the same personal and relational challenges produce the same heartbreaking results.

When we get stuck in this relational quicksand, instead of focusing all of our emotion and energy on accusing and condemning our husbands, God wants us to turn to Him. We must take responsibility for our fuming and festering emotions (which spill out from our hearts when we're squeezed), and confess to God our need for His cleansing. Our forgiveness was purchased at the cross, and it's there that we can find freedom and hope. God can change our hearts as we repent and give us the grace that we need (the power and desire to do His will) to truly respect our husbands in action and attitude. Nancy Wilson speaks of this transforming work of God:

> I have talked with women who were miserable because of the shortcomings they saw in their husbands. I have also seen some of these same women repent of their sin and begin to respect their husbands in concrete ways; their discontent disappears and they become happy, radiant Christian women again. It is amazing! The blessing that results from simple obedience to God's command is wonderful regardless of change in their husbands.

> Wives, instead of focusing on your husband's problems and short-comings, look at what you are supposed to be doing yourself. I have seen the transformation in women as they begin to respect their husbands, and I have no doubt there are great blessings for the husband. It must be a tremendous relief to come home to a sympathetic and encouraging wife, rather than a critical, unhappy, self-centered one. When wives repent of their disobedience and begin to obey God's commands for marriage, blessing always results.[3]

The topic of this section is *Enemies of Respect.* Playing the comparison game is one of those enemies, but there are many others: complaining, self-pity, nagging, discontent, criticizing, ingratitude, rudeness, contempt, and lack of affection.

We can choose whether or not we succumb to these destructive attitudes and actions. Elisabeth Elliot shares an insightful perspective from the point of view of her husband:

> . . . a wife, if she is very generous, may allow that her husband lives up to perhaps eighty percent of her expectations. There is always the other twenty percent that she would like to change, and she may chip away at it for the whole of their married life without reducing it by very much. She may, on the other hand, simply decide to enjoy the eighty percent, and both of them will be happy.[4]

It's a decision. Please ask the Holy Spirit to be at work in your heart to pinpoint the way in which your disrespect shows up in your relationship with your husband. Ask God to renew your respect and to make your heart tender toward your husband. It is in you, his wife, that he should be able to find a place of unconditional acceptance and emotional safety. Confession and repentance will open up our hearts to that supernaturally transforming work of God. He will be faithful to perform it.

Respect and Communication

I was preparing supper one evening when my preschool son, Andy, came into the kitchen with a complaint about his younger brother. I continued stirring at the stove as he earnestly argued his case like a pint-sized prosecutor. He must have recognized that my focus and concern wasn't all that it could have been; he stopped in mid-sentence, raised his voice, and exclaimed, "Mom, listen to me with your eyes!"

Without fully understanding it, Andy was experiencing a relational truth: someone may be talking and someone may be hearing, but that doesn't mean that communication is taking place. By my position (turned toward the stove), my lack of eye contact (watching what I was stirring), and my unresponsiveness (distracted by trying to get dinner ready), Andy knew that he didn't have the sympathetic understanding that he was seeking. He had my ear, but not my heart.

It has been estimated that more than 70% of communication in a marriage is non-verbal. It is true that you can talk without communicating, but you can also speak loudly and clearly without talking. Think about what it must do to our husbands to receive from us a constant diet of eye rolling, sighing, shrugging, and even sneering. Nothing will more surely or quickly undermine the intimacy in a marriage.

On the other hand, think about the power of the following non-verbal communication: eye contact, open and responsive countenance, full attention, and physical affection. A man who receives these positive messages of acceptance and warmth will be a husband whose heart is open and receptive to his wife. It will be a heart in which intimacy can grow and flourish.

I had so much to learn about respectful non-verbal communication when I got married. But I had even more to learn about verbal communication. God was patient and persistent in teaching this stubborn and prideful wife the important lessons of watching my tone, watching my timing, and watching my temper. I wanted to be able to express myself whenever and however my emotions dictated, but my way was a miserable failure.

God taught me that my tone was just as important as my words. Sarcasm is just one of the sinful tones that can chip away at respect (I once heard sarcasm described as "surgery with a chainsaw"). God further taught me that carefully choosing the timing for a critical conversation is a respectful act of love. My way was to meet my unsuspecting husband at the door with an emotional outburst at the end of a particularly trying day. God also taught me to watch my temper. Proverbs 15:1 tells us that *"a gentle answer turns away wrath, but a harsh word stirs up anger."* I've come to believe and experience that a gentle answer turns away the wrath of the hearer *and* the speaker.

The book of Proverbs offers needful wisdom in the art of respectful and gracious communication:

> *Where there are many words, transgression is unavoidable, but he who restrains his lips is wise* (Proverbs 10:19).
>
> *The heart of the righteous ponders how to answer, but the mouth of the wicked pours out evil things* (Proverbs 15:28).
>
> *Pleasant words are a honeycomb, sweet to the soul and healing to the bones* (Proverbs 16:24).
>
> *A fool does not delight in understanding, but only in revealing his own mind* (Proverbs 18:2).
>
> *He who gives an answer before he hears, it is folly and shame to him* (Proverbs 18:13).

Matthew 12:34b tells us that we must take full responsibility for our words: *"For the mouth speaks out of that which fills the heart."*

My words reveal the contents of *my* heart. As wives, we must answer these questions: What fills my heart? Is it disrespect or respect? Is it wisdom or foolishness? God is in the business of transforming our hearts. It is a supernatural work, and He, the author of wisdom and respect, has the power to change us.

The Men Speak

It was at this point in the chapter that I was going to make suggestions about practical ways to show respect to our husbands: listening well, offering encouragement, expressing thanks, showing affection, and not using sex as a bargaining tool. However, that began to seem a little presumptuous. Telling you how to respect your husband might be somewhat like trying to teach you Chinese when I've never visited the country or taken a Chinese language lesson.

So, with the Holy Spirit's prompting, I decided that the best way to make practical suggestions would be to ask lots of husbands for their ideas on the subject. The following comments are samples of the honest and heart-felt responses from the men who took the time to answer my survey. The first question that they answered was: **What is one thing your wife does that makes you feel respected in your marriage?** Here are their unedited and thought-provoking responses:

> "Any compliments, expressions of gratitude or words of encouragement are always appreciated and a morale booster for me."
>
> "She asks my opinion and advice in the important things of life and compliments me to others."
>
> "When she leaves me a note in my lunch box stating that she loves me."
>
> "She listens to me and offers her perspective on my issues and what concerns my world."

"My wife engages in things that are important to me and that I enjoy pursuing, and that makes me more willing to do the same for her. She trusts me and believes in me. She forgives my failings so much that we can laugh at them together without hurt feelings or lingering resentment. This frees me to become better instead of being defensive and seeking to be 'right.' She admits when she's wrong and is more critical of herself than me. This makes me all the more willing to build her up and extol her virtues. She understands when I'm out of words, need to clear my brain and need companionship. She knows me and accepts me always. She's my biggest fan."

"She fully trusts me in every aspect of our lives."

"She is always faithful to pray for me and with me, especially in times of need."

"Agrees to do something I would like to do when it's not necessarily what she would like to do."

"She tells other people about things I'm good at."

"She is intuitive and encourages me at the right time. She puts aside her interest to support my endeavors and plans. A kind touch periodically also helps. She acknowledges my position within the family."

"She asks my advice on things."

"I like it when I know my wife has spoken highly of me in front of others. When she does not put me down or say disrespectful things about me to other people."

"When she believes in me; forgives me and never tears me down in public."

"When she has a willingness to follow my lead, especially in difficult situations."

The second question on the survey was: **What is one thing your wife could do that would make you feel more respected in your marriage?** Again, the responses are unedited:

"Be less combative and more respectful in her tone of voice when we are talking."

"She does this sometimes already, but you know us guys, we have HUGE egos. I think I would say when she compliments me in front of others."

"Listening to what I have to say."

"Thank me for providing for our family more regularly."

"Make a concerted effort to share more quality time together."

"Support my efforts by complimenting me or offering words of encouragement. Be appreciative of efforts I make to support her. Build me up to others & my family."

"Trust me a little more."

"Speak words of affirmation. Want to go out on dates more."

"Seek my opinion more often when issues arise concerning the kids. At times she attacks issues without my input."

The third question was: **When do you feel most disrespected in your marriage?**

> "When my wife is the least interested in me, expresses the most dissatisfaction with who she perceives me to be as a person and least appreciative of what I do to provide for our family."
>
> "Having to 'beg' for certain marital obligations, where when the shoe is on the other foot with other types of marital obligations, my wife would be seriously offended if I made her 'beg' or jump through hoops for those."
>
> "When she complains (to me or others) about my faults (actual, legitimate, or perceived)."
>
> "Mainly it is a tone she uses on occasions that sounds as if she thinks I am stupid when she asks questions and hears my response or responds to a question I have asked—not often enough to be an issue, but would not miss that tone at all."
>
> "When my wife presumes something about me in front of others."
>
> "When she goes off on a tangent without discussing it first if it affects what we are trying to accomplish as a family or in raising the kids."
>
> "When no one acknowledges what I do for the family."
>
> "My wife quit telling me, 'I told you so,' long ago."
>
> "Not listen when I talk."

"If my wife disagrees with me in front of others or demeans me because she does not agree."

"When my wife uses her cell phone (talking, texting, answering e-mail) when we are having dinner, out on a date, alone. I feel that others are more important to her than me."

"When I'm not included in decisions."

"When I ask her to do something and it doesn't get taken care of, but this is usually not on purpose, and is probably a communication problem."

An Excellent Wife

Proverbs 31 depicts for us the qualities of an excellent wife. For 22 verses, the virtues of this woman are described and extolled. It is instructive that the first 3 verses of this well-known passage portray first and foremost a woman who respects her husband:

An excellent wife, who can find?
For her worth is far above jewels.
The heart of her husband trusts in her,
And he will have no lack of gain.
She does him good and not evil
All the days of her life (verses 10-12).

I believe it says in just a few words exactly what was being expressed in the previous survey responses. It essentially boils down to one husband's comment: "She's my biggest fan."

Before I leave this chapter, I want to mention one final and vitally important point. If you have children, it is crucial for them to see a mom who respects their father. This has such long-term implications for your children. Habitual disrespect will erode their sense of security, and it will also influence the way in which they relate to others. Children desperately need to respect their fathers, and you can be sure that they will follow your lead.

Current television sit-coms and movies make a sport of humiliating men and minimizing the significant role of husbands and fathers in the life of a family. What seems to be a lighthearted and innocent comedy can become an insidious evil when it is replicated in our homes. Our young sons and daughters are having their identities shaped by our words, behaviors, and ways of relating. As Christian women, we must take seriously the goal of modeling for our daughters the respectful behavior that Scripture describes. And for the welfare of our young sons, we must respect the father whom they so profoundly desire to admire and emulate.

For some of you, learning to respect your husband may seem to be an impossible goal. But you can be confident that for every one of God's instructions, His grace is abundantly available for the task at hand. He doesn't leave us to accomplish it in our own strength. He understands our frailty, and He delights in providing power in our weakness. Turn to Him, count on Him, confess to Him your need, and then obey Him by His grace:

> . . . *And all of you, clothe yourselves with humility toward one another, for God is opposed to the proud, but gives grace to the humble. Humble yourselves, therefore, under the mighty hand of God, that He may exalt you at the proper time, casting all your anxiety upon Him, because He cares for you"* (1 Peter 5:5b-7).

[1] Carolyn Mahaney, *Feminine Appeal* (Wheaton, Illinois: Crossway Books, 2004), 148.
[2] Gary Thomas, *Sacred Marriage* (Grand Rapids, Michigan: Zondervan, 2000), 69.
[3] Nancy Wilson, *The Fruit of Her Hands* (Moscow, Idaho: Canon Press, 1997), 32-33.
[4] Elisabeth Elliot, *Love Has a Price Tag* (Ann Arbor, Michigan: Servant Books, 1979), 97.

Chapter Eight

Forgiveness is a Choice, Not a Feeling

Years ago I was teaching a Sunday school class of high schoolers. We were discussing the description of love in 1 Corinthians 13. I asked each of them to silently read verses four through six and to write down the characteristic of love that was the biggest challenge for them. There wasn't a big variety of answers—overwhelmingly the kids wrote down *"love . . . does not take into account a wrong suffered"* (verse 5). I had wondered if that would be the case, because that was my own answer.

When we are wronged, we take it into account. We may even keep a mental file when we are wronged repeatedly. It's difficult to set aside our feelings when we've been offended. It's especially challenging when our husbands are the offenders.

There is a series of verses in Proverbs that describes the "contentious" wife. She is, no doubt, a woman who takes into account a wrong suffered and whose heart is a safe haven for unforgiveness:

> *. . . the contentions of a wife are a constant dripping* (Proverbs 19:13b).

Solomon doesn't stop there—it gets a bit more personal:

> *It is better to live in a corner of a roof, than in a house shared with a contentious woman* (Proverbs 21:9).

Ouch! It gets worse:

> *It is better to live in a desert land, than with a contentious and vexing woman* (Proverbs 21:19).

A desert? Really? But wait, there's more:

> *A constant dripping on a day of steady rain and a contentious woman are alike* (Proverbs 27:15).

Solomon doesn't cut these women any slack. Earlier in chapter 18, he shares another thought about *contentions:*

> *. . . And contentions are like the bars of a castle* (Proverbs 18:19b).

I think we get the picture. A contentious wife is eager to argue her case and prove her point. A contentious wife holds onto unforgiveness until her heart has been hardened over the years by hostility and resentment. Love loses the battle to bitterness. And her contentiousness makes her home into a prison for the rest of her family.

There are many opportunities in our marriages to allow a root of bitterness to grow in our hearts. How do we guard against becoming a contentious and resentful wife? God has provided the way in His great gift of forgiveness—the forgiveness that is offered *to* us in Christ *and* the forgiveness that flows *through* us by His grace.

God's Forgiveness Toward Us

> *And so, as those who have been chosen of God, holy and beloved, put on a heart of compassion, kindness, humility, gentleness and patience; bearing with one another, and forgiving each other, whoever has a complaint against anyone; just as the Lord forgave you, so also should you* (Colossians 3:12-13).

If we, as these verses instruct, are to forgive just as we've been forgiven, then we need to understand the fullness of God's forgiveness to us. It is, after all, the model of the forgiveness that we are to offer to others.

God's Forgiveness Can't Be Earned

First of all, God's forgiveness is in no way obtained by any effort on our part. Take this to heart and rejoice that you don't have to work for your forgiveness:

> *. . . A [woman] is not justified by the works of the Law but through faith in Christ Jesus, even we have believed in Christ Jesus, that we may be justified by faith in Christ, and not by the works of the Law; since by the works of the Law shall no flesh be justified* (Galatians 2:16).

We don't have to jump through hoops to gain God's favor. Our forgiveness is not attained by a check-list. Our forgiveness was obtained at the cross when Jesus shed His blood to pay the penalty for our sin. That's it. For those who belong to Christ, the penalty has been paid for every sin we have or ever will commit.

You may ask what that means in regard to our daily sin. If the penalty for sin required the death of God's Son, then doesn't our daily sin have some consequesnce? Does God just turn His head and not pay attention? The account of Jesus washing the disciples' feet gives helpful insight into this matter. After Jesus had eaten His last meal with His disciples, He poured water into a basin and began washing their feet. John 13:6-10 records this event:

> *And so He came to Simon Peter. He said to Him, "Lord, do you wash my feet?" Jesus answered and said to him, "What I do you do not realize now,but you shall understand hereafter." Peter said to Him, "Never shall you wash my feet!" Jesus answered him, "If I do not wash you, you have no part with Me." Simon Peter said to Him, "Lord, not my feet only, but also my hands and my head." Jesus said to him, "He who has bathed needs only to wash His feet, but is completely clean; and you are clean . . ."*

The full "bath" of salvation is a one-time event. My salvation gives me new life and the Holy Spirit comes to indwell me. The penalty for my sin is paid in full and forever.

However, I still sin. When that happens, I need my "feet washed." My sin grieves the Holy Spirit. It is an offense against God and disrupts the fellowship I have with Him and others. I must confess my sin according to 1 John 1:9: *"If we confess our sins, He is faithful and righteous to forgive us our sins and to cleanse us from all unrighteousness."*

Once again, God's forgiveness is not based on my performance. It's based entirely on the death of Christ which fully paid the penalty of guilt for my sin. Once I have confessed my sin and repented, then my fellowship with God is restored. (I didn't lose my salvation when I sinned, and I didn't regain my salvation when I confessed my sin.) The "bath" of salvation happens once, but the "foot cleansing" for daily offenses is necessary every time I sin.

How do I apply this truth in my marriage? The sub-title for this section is *God's Forgiveness Can't Be Earned.* If I am to forgive as God forgives, then I must freely offer forgiveness to my husband. So often, wives withhold forgiveness until their husbands jump through the proper hoops; in effect, they must earn their way back into the full acceptance of their wives.

Our standing before God was secured at the cross. That never changes. My husband's "standing" with me was secured with my wedding vows. It was with those vows that I fully committed my life to him. That never changes.

When I sin against God, as I said earlier, my fellowship with Him is disrupted, but my standing with Him does not change. The same thing happens in my relationship with my husband when he sins against me. Our intimacy is disturbed, but our commitment doesn't alter. I cannot withhold forgiveness from my husband until he performs according to my ten-point checklist. My husband should not have to *earn* my forgiveness. That really wouldn't even be real forgiveness;

it would simply be having my emotions stroked according to my own desires and demands.

You may think that forgiveness is letting your husband "off the hook." You may want to withhold forgiveness until he has learned his lesson or until he has paid the full price of his offense. It is our natural tendency to want our offender to hurt as much as we have been hurt, and that often includes our desire to make our husbands earn our forgiveness. Does forgiveness mean, then, that the wounds of an offense are immediately forgotten?

Tara Klena Barthel and Judy Dabler offer an invaluable insight in their explanation of the distinction between reconciliation and restoration:

> Think of the analogy of a broken bone. If a leg is broken, the doctor sets the bone and the gap is healed (reconciled). This is what happens when someone confesses to us and we forgive [him]. Yet in the same way that a freshly set bone is not ready to bear weight, a broken relationship, newly reconciled, often needs time and help to be fully restored. A broken bone might need a cast or physical therapy for complete restoration. The same thing happens to a relationship following reconciliation. It often takes prayer, time, and focused effort to build trust back into a formerly broken relationship. A good rule of thumb: the greater the fracture, the longer the recovery time. Just as a healed bone that never bears weight will never grow stronger, relationships that are avoided or neglected will never grow stronger. God's grace and mercy enable us to strengthen reconciled relationships . . . . Reconciliation [forgiveness] is an event, but restoration is a process . . . .[1]

Again, God's grace is a necessary ingredient in this process. We need His help to forgive. I can pretend to forgive, gloss over or excuse an offense, or bury the hurt deep in my heart. I can do all of these things in my own strength. But I need God's grace to truly forgive. It is not an emotion, but a choice that I can make by God's grace. When I forgive my husband, I am trusting God to work in his life to bring about any necessary change. I am trusting God to provide the necessary grace that we need to fully restore our relationship. Pastor and author John MacArthur says,

> Forgiveness is first of all an act of the will. It is not hypocrisy to will forgiveness when the emotions are screaming for vengeance. Be obedient to the Lord regardless of how you feel. If you refuse to harbor spite or dwell on the offense, evil emotions will be starved. Moreover, the Lord Himself will set your heart right. Right emotions will eventually come if you surrender to Him.[2]

I cannot emphasize strongly enough that one of God's purposes for marriage is to use it as a context to show us how much we need Him. He wants us to come to understand His abundant grace and the strength it can provide for us in our weakness. He wants us to understand the depth of forgiveness that He offers to us. His plan is for us to deeply grasp our need for the gospel: we don't deserve God's grace, but He freely offers it to us because of the death of His perfect Son on our behalf.

When these truths begin to penetrate our hearts, then we become more willing, sometimes even eager, to offer the same forgiveness to our husbands when they offend us. We realize that we are no different than they are; we're sinners, too, and our sins are equally as offensive, requiring from God the same payment—the death of our Savior. The process of forgiving our husbands must take us to the cross. It is there that we find the freedom to forgive as we have been forgiven.

God's Forgiveness is Motivated by Love

Romans 5:8 says, *"But God demonstrates His own love toward us, in that while we were yet sinners, Christ died for us."* God didn't start loving us after we cleaned up our act. We talked about love in Chapter One—just like love, forgiveness is not a feeling. Both love and forgiveness are choices I make by the grace of God.

When I am in a circumstance in which I need to forgive my husband, one of the love choices I must make is to take responsibility for my thoughts and emotions. Typically, if left to my own devices, I allow my thoughts to run rampant: "I can't believe that he did that." "What was he thinking?" "Doesn't he get it?" "He makes me so mad."

And those are just the beginning. My thoughts are off and running. The problem is that I'm not putting up any roadblocks, or even speed bumps, to halt or slow down my destructive thinking. I'm allowing my thoughts to whip me into an emotional frenzy—a virtual Tasmanian devil ready to devour my unsuspecting and unprepared husband. This is not a choice of love—well, maybe it's a choice of love for myself, but certainly not for my husband.

Dear wives, our thoughts can take us down such dangerous paths. Our energy and emotions become focused on the offense and the perpetrators of the offense—our husbands. The tape in our head plays over and over, and we careen down the path of relational destruction. It's time to put on the brakes. Instead of focusing all of our attention on our husbands and their offenses toward us, we must refocus our hearts and minds to recognize that our responsibility is to give attention to our response. We cannot change our husbands, but we can choose to change the direction of our thoughts and emotions.

The story of Joseph in the book of Genesis is such an astounding example of true and costly forgiveness. Joseph's brothers had committed unthinkable acts of betrayal against their brother. Yet when, by God's sovereignty, he was reunited with his brothers in Egypt, he *chose* to forgive them. John Calvin offers this insight:

> Had Joseph kept his thoughts fixed on the treachery of his brethren, he never could have resumed fraternal affection for them. But turning toward the Lord, he forgot the injury, and was so inclined to mildness and

> mercy, that he even voluntarily comforts his brethren, telling them, *"Be not grieved nor angry with yourselves that ye sold me hither; for God did send me before you to preserve life"* (Genesis 45:5).[3]

If there is anyone who could ever have justified a refusal to forgive, it would have been Joseph. He could easily and legally have had his brothers imprisoned or killed. Yet He recognized God's hand in the events of his life, and he made the choice to forgive and love.

This is so difficult. It is a spiritual battle. We must avail ourselves of God's grace (that is one reason I included 2 chapters on God's grace—it is *the* essential ingredient in a godly marriage). He can give us the power and the desire to take control of our thoughts as we are instructed to do in 2 Corinthians 10:5b: *". . . and we are taking every thought captive to the obedience of Christ."*

This is an act of love and can only be accomplished by God's grace. It is a necessary step on the way to forgiveness. Please understand that thoughts are not private. The thoughts we dwell on will become apparent in our behavior. That is why it is so important to evaluate our thoughts by God's Word. Our sinful and destructive thinking needs to be exposed by the truth of Scripture.

The Truth says that God forgave me while I was still a sinner. My debt of sin was one I could never repay. The Truth is that God willingly and completely forgave me. I am to forgive in the same way that I was forgiven. God's motivation was love, and His love is available to me by His grace. It is His desire that His love be manifested through me in forgiveness toward my husband.

God's Forgiveness is Complete

God's forgiveness toward me is complete. He doesn't reserve a little wrath in case I don't quite meet up to His expectations. He doesn't take His forgiveness back when I fail once again. His forgiveness restores and cleanses me. And I am to forgive in the same way.

Isaiah 43:25 speaks of the fullness of God's forgiveness: *"I, even I, am the one who wipes out your transgressions for my own sake; and I will not remember your sins."* John MacArthur explains that this verse does not mean that God forgets our sin; He cannot forget anything: "Obviously God, who is omniscient, has not lost His memory of our transgressions. Rather, He refuses to call them to mind. He promises not to bring them up."[4]

Matthew Henry says of this verse that it is "as if the great God would teach us that forgiving injuries is the best way to keep ourselves from being wearied with them."[5] When we haul around the heavy burden of unforgiveness, it is wearying. Unforgiveness fertilizes the soil of our hearts so that a root of bitterness can grow deep and strong. The peaceful fruit of righteousness is overshadowed and choked, and our lives are drained of spiritual vitality.

In 1861 Charles H. Spurgeon preached a sermon entitled "It Is Finished" in which he eloquently summarizes the glorious truth of the completeness of God's forgiveness:

> . . . The satisfaction which [Jesus] rendered to the justice of God was finished. The debt was now, to the last farthing, all discharged. The atonement and propitiation were made once for all, and forever, by the one offering made in Jesus' body on the tree. There was a cup; Hell was in it, the Savior drank it—not a sip and then a pause, not a draught and then a ceasing, but He drained it till there is not a dreg left for any of His people! The great ten-thronged whip of the law was worn out upon His back; there is no lash left with which to smite one for whom Christ died! The great cannonade of God's Justice has exhausted all its ammunition; there is nothing left to be hurled against a child of God! Sheathed is your sword, O Justice! Silenced is your thunder, O Law! There remains nothing now of all the griefs, and pains, and agonies which chosen sinners ought to have suffered for their

sins, for Christ has endured all for His own Beloved, and "it is finished."[6]

God offers complete forgiveness, and it is His plan for us to do the same. When we offer complete forgiveness, we are promising to "remember it no more." That doesn't mean that we forget it (though we may over time). It means that we will refuse to bring it up to our husbands or others in order to use it against them in some way. It means that we will trust God to work in us to bring complete restoration by His grace and in His timing. And in the meantime, we will be active in our love toward our husbands, taking responsibility for our thoughts and emotions, and being patient as God works in both of us to conform us into the image of His Son.

An Attitude of Forgiveness

Do you know someone with whom you are always a little uncomfortable because she seems to have a chip on her shoulder? You may feel that you're constantly "walking on eggshells" around her. A genuine friendship is highly unlikely, because you can't be completely open with her, because you feel like you're being judged in many of the things you say and do. I would say that this is a person who does not have an "attitude of forgiveness."

The *act* of forgiveness is crucial when an offense has been committed, but it is also essential to be characterized by an *attitude* of forgiveness—a general willingness and openness to look at life and circumstances from the point of view of another—particularly your husband. An attitude of forgiveness means that I carry around in my heart the perspective that my husband and I are on the same team. I do my best to refrain from assigning to him my interpretation of his actions and motives. I am conscious of any tendency to be "touchy" or hyper-sensitive. When it is possible, I "cut him some slack."

It is so easy to be ready to pounce on our husbands' every little blunder. Scripture instructs us *"to pursue peace with all men"* (Hebrews 12:14), and that certainly includes our spouses. Romans

14:19 affirms that same idea: *"So then let us pursue the things which make for peace and the building up of one another."* That word *"pursue"* doesn't give us much wiggle-room. It should be our aim and objective to achieve and maintain peace in our relationships with our husbands. Sometimes that will involve honest and fruitful communication; sometimes it may involve turning the other cheek.

This pursuit of peace is particularly important when our husbands make unintentional mistakes or errors which inconvenience us in some way. This may include forgetting an important date, getting directions wrong, failing to successfully complete a repair job, or not noticing a new haircut or outfit.

These things are not sins or malicious deeds. However, in cases such as these, wives can be quick to find fault with husbands who fail to act according to their standard of performance. This lack of an attitude of forgiveness shows up in our words, actions, and attitudes. Please don't think that an impatient shrug or roll of the eyes goes unnoticed by our husbands.

These occasions are ultimately from the hand of God. He knows how much we need to change, and He knows how to accomplish it. We need lots of practice! To gain a gracious and forgiving attitude toward our husbands, we must recognize the circumstances that God provides for the purpose of pruning away our prickly thorns and unhealthy branches. The process may be painful, but we can trust that beautiful and life-giving fruit will be produced in our lives and in our marriages. Elisabeth Elliot speaks of this sanctifying and transformational process:

> We cannot make ourselves holy. But when we surrender ourselves to the Lord, learning day by day to treat all that comes to us with peace of soul and firm conviction that His will governs all, He will see to our growth in grace. He will so govern the events in our lives, down to the smallest detail, as to provide for us the conditions which may make us fruitful.[7]

God wants to grow in us an attitude of forgiveness. At the beginning of this chapter I quoted Colossians 3:12, 13, which speaks of compassion, kindness, humility, gentleness, patience, and bearing with one another. There is no better description of what characterizes an attitude of forgiveness. Accomplishing it is a process, and it comes by God's grace. Open your heart to God's work in you, presenting to Him good soil in which He can cultivate the holy fruit of forgiveness.

One More Thought

This chapter and book were written for wives. It may seem that I'm putting all the responsibilities of marriage on your shoulders. If I were writing to husbands, I would say many of the same things—perhaps even more. But I'm not writing to husbands; I'm writing to you, and my prayer is that you'll take to heart the content of this important chapter on forgiveness. Ask God for His grace to help you to obey the truths of His Word. And then pray and trust Him to work in the heart of your husband. He can do what you can't.

[1] Tara Klena Barthel & Judy Dabler, 113, 114.

[2] John MacArthur, *Answering the Hard Questions About Forgiveness* (Panorama City, California: Grace to You, 2002), 8.

[3] Nancy Guthrie, *Be Still, My Soul* (Wheaton, Illinois: Crossway, 2010), 50.

[4] MacArthur, 7.

[5] Matthew Henry, 890.

[6] *Spurgeon Gems – Sermons of Charles Spurgeon & Other Treasures of God's Truth.* December 17 2011. <http://www.spurgeongems.org>.

[7] Elisabeth Elliot, *A Path Through Suffering,* 59.

Chapter Nine

God is Enough

Unlike many of my friends, when I graduated from college, I wasn't planning my wedding. I hadn't even met my future husband. It was the opinion of some that I had lost my greatest opportunity for finding happiness in this life. In the next few months I would be a bridesmaid several times. It was tempting to believe that I had missed out on my happily ever after.

To some extent, every bride looks to her young husband to fulfill her hopes and dreams. Undoubtedly, her anticipation of wedded bliss has been a deep part of her heart's desire for many years. This expectation is often a recipe for disappointment and disillusionment. God has never created a man who could live up to the lofty ideal of girlhood dreams and adolescent crushes.

One of the greatest gifts wives can give to their husbands is to relieve them of the responsibility of being everything to them. Husbands cannot do it. It is too high a standard. They are, after all, just men. They haven't been given a witty romantic script, and they cannot produce a perfect ending in just less than two hours. They live in real life, and they have real-life weaknesses and foibles. They have annoying habits and inexplicable idiosyncrasies—just as we do.

Dearest wives, we must grant permission to our husbands to be imperfect. We must accept the irrefutable fact: a marriage is comprised of two sinners. There is only One who is perfect, and He is our Creator God. His love for us is perfect, His care for us is absolute, and His understanding of us is complete.

I think Psalm 139 says it better than I ever could. As you read this passage, realize that these words are not meant to be about David the Psalmist only; they're fully true for you and for me. It is an intimately personal psalm, and you need to construe it in that way.

Make it your prayer to your Heavenly Father; read it aloud slowly, and carefully consider the words as you speak them:

> *O Lord, you have searched me and known me!*
> *You know when I sit down and when I rise up;*
> *You discern my thoughts from afar.*
> *You search out my path and my lying down*
> *and are acquainted with all my ways.*
> *Even before a word is on my tongue,*
> *behold, O Lord, You know it altogether.*
> *You hem me in, behind and before,*
> *and lay Your hand upon me.*
> *Such knowledge is too wonderful for me;*
> *it is high; I cannot attain it . . . .*
> *For you formed my inward parts;*
> *You knitted me together in my mother's womb.*
> *I praise you, for I am fearfully and wonderfully made.*
> *Wonderful are your works;*
> *My soul knows it very well.*
> *My frame was not hidden from you,*
> *When I was being made in secret,*
> *intricately woven in the depths of the earth.*
> *Your eyes saw my unformed substance;*
> *in your book were written, every one of them,*
> *the days that were formed for me,*
> *when as yet there was none of them.*
> *How precious to me are your thoughts, O God!*
> *How vast is the sum of them!*
> *If I would count them, they are more than the sand*
> (Psalm 139:1-6; 13-18a).

This God created you and loves you more than you will ever know (perhaps in Heaven we'll fathom the depth of His love). He discerns your thoughts and understands your ways. He says this about you: *"Can a woman forget her nursing child, that she should have no compassion on the son of her womb? Even these may forget, yet I will not forget you. Behold, 'I have engraved you on the palms of my hands . . ."* (Isaiah 49:15-16a).

God's intention and desire is to be in a deep, real, personal, and reciprocal relationship with you. This should be impossible—we're talking about the Creator of the universe. But do you remember the torn veil (Matthew 27:51)? When Jesus gave His life on the cross, the veil of the temple was torn in two from top to bottom, and all the fullness of a new life with God was opened up to those who put their faith in Christ. His death paid the full penalty for the guilt of our sin. Grace, not guilt, now defines our relationship with God.

The author of Hebrews tells us that we can now *"draw near with confidence to the throne of grace . . ."* (4:16). This confidence is not in ourselves, but in that perfect sacrifice that was made on our behalf at Calvary. Rejoice in this blessed and historical fact: the foundation and basis for your relationship with God is not in any way provided by you; it was completely and eternally accomplished by Christ.

Charles Wesley celebrates this truth in one of his hymns which has become an Easter favorite:

> Love's redeeming work is done,
> fought the fight, the battle won.
> Death in vain forbids Him rise;
> Christ has opened paradise.
> ALLELUIA!

I am emphasizing this, because it is imperative that we have an assurance that God is favorably inclined toward us—He loves us. So many women are doubtful about this glorious truth, because they believe that they must in some way measure up to God's love.

If you're not convinced of God's eternal love for you based on the death of Christ for you, then you'll be forever tempted to find your heart's desire in someone or something else. If you put your hope for fulfillment in your husband, the weight of that burden will defeat him and crush your marriage. God does delight to bless us with love in our marriages, but our deep soul-satisfaction will never be found in anything or anyone but God alone.

Three Questions I Must Ask Myself

God wants our whole hearts. This is not negotiable. In 2 Chronicles 16:9, Hanani the seer confronts Asa, King of Judah, because Asa had relied on a foreign king for support instead of seeking God. In his challenge to Asa, Hanani speaks this truth: *"For the eyes of the Lord move to and fro throughout the earth that He may strongly support those whose heart is completely His . . . ."*

How can you determine if you're placing your full trust and hope in God? How do you know if He has your full heart? Please ask God to help you honestly answer the following three questions. They will give you insight into your motivations and desires.

"Where Do I Find My Peace?"

This question may be answered differently at various times in our lives. Several years ago I found out that my answer was not what it should have been. One Sunday morning as I was getting ready for church, I heard an unfamiliar thud in my sons' bathroom. I didn't think much about it (unexplained thuds are a way of life when you have three sons), but after a couple of minutes, I realized that the thud had been followed by complete silence. Something in my mother's heart sounded an alarm. I rushed from my bedroom and out into the hall outside of my boys' bathroom. I saw that my youngest son's bedroom door was open, so I knew that he was the one in the bathroom.

With a vague sense of anxiety, I knocked on the door and called out his name, "Philip, are you OK?" No answer. More frantic knocking. "Philip, ARE YOU OK?" Still no answer. I tried the doorknob which was locked. I yelled for my oldest son Andy to come immediately (Rob, my husband, was already at church). Andy ran upstairs from his bedroom as I explained to him that Philip was not answering my call.

Because it was a knob for which we had no key, we quickly determined that Andy would have to force his way into the bathroom. He rammed his shoulder into the door, and as it flew open, the mirror on the inside of the door shattered on top of my unconscious son who was sprawled face-down on the floor.

There are no words to describe the utter terror of that moment. We immediately called 911 which beckoned a police car, fire truck and ambulance. In the meantime, my husband had rushed home in response to my distraught phone call. In all of this time, Philip still had not regained consciousness.

As the EMTs struggled amidst all of the glass to get Philip onto a stretcher, he slowly began to come around. My relief was short-lived, however, because it was obvious that he was looking at us with blank eyes and absolutely no recognition. As he began to aggressively resist the attempts of the medics to strap him onto the stretcher, my dismay grew to panic. What was wrong with my son?

After several hours in the emergency room, we left with no firm answers. One possibility offered was that Philip had had a seizure. That seemed so out of the blue; Philip was strong and healthy and had never had any physical or medical problems. We left with uneasiness, but thankfulness that though he was completely exhausted, Philip had seemingly recovered.

It was several months later that this event repeated itself. There was no denying this time that Philip had had a seizure. What followed was months of testing, blood work, ER visits, and appointments with a neurologist who initially misdiagnosed the type of seizure disorder that Philip had. He was prescribed a medication that actually made him worse. He spent many nights with mild (jerking arms or legs) to severe (generalized) seizure activity which frequently kept us up most or all of the night. It was a discouraging, exhausting, and often desperate time.

Now to return to the first question: *Where do I find my peace?* It was during this time that God revealed to me that a huge portion of my peace was found in the well-being of my sons. How did I discover that? Well, it was obvious. The physical health of my youngest son was being threatened . . . and I had no peace. I had never before experienced the depth of anxiety and fear that I was living with as each day drew to a close (all of Philip's seizure activity took place after he went to bed or just upon waking). As day turned to night, a dark sense of dread would descend upon me. Would this be another night of frightening and menacing seizure activity?

One night I sat on the floor in the hallway outside Philip's closed bedroom door. It had become his routine to come get me when he thought he might have a seizure—he would feel "twitchy" and know that he was vulnerable. However, my great fear was that he would have a sudden seizure and be unable to call for help. As I sat listening intently outside of Philip's door, I begged God to take away his seizures or to at least take them from Philip and give them to me.

I have never heard an audible voice from God, but the Holy Spirit unmistakably spoke to my heart: *"Susan, you have prayed for your son to grow into a godly man; would you have me take away the very instrument I am using to accomplish that purpose?"* With a weary and broken heart, I surrendered the well-being of my son to God for His purposes. Peace flooded my heart, and I realized that my previous prayers for peace had been nothing more than desperate pleas to escape from our suffering. It had been my belief that peace could only come when my son was strong and healthy. I had seriously underestimated the grace and peace of God.

We look to many different sources for peace: close friends, physical and emotional well-being, steady employment, healthy bank account. It is completely understandable that a supportive marriage may be our hope for peace. When all of these areas of our lives are positive, then it is easy to enjoy the peace that ensues. But God offers a deeper and more abiding peace, *"the peace which surpasses all understanding"* (Philippians 4:7). It is not a peace tied to people or circumstances, but a peace that comes from the very heart of God.

When the peace in our marriages is disturbed, the underlying message in our prayers for peace could really sound something like this:

> Lord, please remove all the difficulties and challenges in my marriage. You see, I would really prefer not having to grow up and change. It's inconvenient and difficult. If I have to grow and change, I will have to depend fully on you. If you could just change my husband, then I could stay the same, and I wouldn't need you so much, and I wouldn't have to do the hard work of growing up. So Lord . . . please either take the challenges away, or just change my husband. Either will be fine. Thanks.

The truth is that we don't want a *peace that surpasses understanding.* We want a peace that we can control and a peace that doesn't require any hard (or *heart*) work.

A wife with a heart of peace is a great gift and blessing to her husband. God can grant us this great peace—it is a process, often daunting, but He is infinitely patient to teach us. Elisabeth Elliot says it this way:

> Each time God gives us a hard lesson, He desires to give us Himself. If we open our hands to receive the lesson, we open our hearts to receive Him . . . . The Everlasting Arms are always underneath us, the everlasting love always surrounds us.[1]

"How Do I Fill My Heart?"

I grew up in a little town—population 1414. A sign proclaiming this bit of information was erected on the outskirts of the city limits and remained unchanged for years. Our town boasted a small downtown library. My brother, sister and I would walk to the library every Saturday during our summer break from school to check out a week's worth of books. I don't know how they felt about this event, but I loved it. The library was damp and had a pungent, mildewy odor. To this day, I still fondly remember that tiny library whenever I venture into a dark and dank cellar.

After a sweltering walk back home with our arms full of books, I would rush to my room and climb up on my bed. It was always a difficult chore to choose which book I would read first. When I'd made my decision, the grieving process would begin. I knew ahead of time how involved I would become with the protagonist and the rest of the characters, and I really started missing them before I'd even begun reading. I would postpone the heartache by opening the book and smelling the musty pages and daydreaming about the pleasure to come. Ugh! This all sounds a bit pathetic and nerdy, but it's true.

This rather embarrassing moment from my past is brought to you because I want to confess that one of the reasons I've always loved books is because they can provide such an emotional boost for my heart. I realized it anew after our family made a move from Kentucky to North Carolina. One of the first things we did was to go to the library in our new city and acquire library cards. We checked out lots of books.

The problem came when I realized (with the Holy Spirit's help) that I was using books to calm the anxiety I had about our boys starting a new school year when they didn't yet have any friends. I was attempting to take the edge off my homesickness by involving myself with the characters in the book I was reading. I was filling my time with books, because I didn't yet have comfortable relationships in our new church. I was using books as an escape. I was relinquishing the availability of God's grace to help me in my adjustment to a new home, and I was escaping instead to a comforting, familiar, and seemingly harmless pastime.

We have many choices available to us in our attempts to fill the vast reservoirs of our hearts: shopping, surfing the internet, vacations, hobbies, Facebook, television—the list is endless. Many of the activities we engage in are not necessarily sinful. But when we use them as a substitute for God and for the work of His grace in our hearts, then they are sinful indeed.

There is a story of a man who tells his little grandson about a ferocious clash between two fighting dogs. In the story, the boy asks his grandfather which dog is going to win the battle. The wise elder answers that the dog who wins is the one who is fed the most. A comparison can obviously be made to the internal battle we encounter when our flesh wages war against our spirit. Galatians 5:17 speaks of this spiritual battle: *"For the flesh sets its desire against the Spirit, and the Spirit against the flesh; for these are in opposition to one another. . . ."*

So, I ask you, how do you fill your heart? In other words, how do you *feed* your heart? Are you routinely feeding your flesh with the things which bring temporary distraction and pleasure? This is definitely an easier path, but in the end it brings spiritual malaise and bondage. Pursuing a life of abiding in Christ and feeding our spirits (meeting with Him in prayer and in His Word, pursuing fellowship with other believers, etc.) is fraught with challenges and trials, but in the end it brings freedom and peace. To be a supportive and godly wife, I must fill my heart with spiritual food to strengthen and equip me for the challenges and pressures which marriage brings. I cannot be the wife God calls me to be if I attempt to subsist on relational fast food.

If you have children, you have likely told them, "No candy before dinner. It'll ruin your appetite." This is true of our spiritual appetites as well. Feeding our spirits with "sweets" will take away our appetite for the nourishing food that God provides. The sweets will eventually make us sick and malnourished, and the pleasure they provide will be short-lived and meaningless. Our priority must be receiving our meals from the Bread of Life: *". . . he who comes to Me shall not hunger, and he who believes in Me shall never thirst"* (John 6:35).

In her book, *Praying God's Word,* Beth Moore says:

> God created us with a cavernous need that we would seek to fill until we found Him. Searching for perfect, unfailing love in anyone else is not only fruitless, it is miserably disappointing and destructive. I am convinced our hearts are not healthy until they have

> been satisfied by the only completely healthy love that exists: the love of God, Himself. The following words by Oswald Chambers are not only written in the front of my Bible, they are engraved deeply in my mind: "No love of the natural heart is safe unless the human heart has been satisfied by God first." We are not free to love in the true intent of the word until we have found love. All of us have looked, but the important question is where? . . . We each have our unmet needs, and we carry them around all day long like an empty cup. In one way or another, we hold out that empty cup to the people in our lives and say, "Can somebody please fill this?" Whether we seek to have our cup filled through approval, affirmation, control, success, or immediate gratification, we are miserable until something is in it. . . . What a heavy yoke is shattered when we awaken in the morning, bring our hearts, minds, and souls and all their "needs" to the Great Soul-ologist, offer Him our empty cups, and ask Him to fill them with Himself! [2]

"Where Do I Run in the Tough Times?"

My husband's first pastorate was in Yankeetown, Florida (we had never heard of it either). There were definitely many more wild animals there than people. My oldest son and I took pictures of the various creatures that found their way into our yard: foxes, deer, scorpions, and fire ants, to name a few. Periodically, on the road leading to our house, we'd observe the road kill remains of a boar or any number of troublesomely long snakes. My husband spied an alligator or two on fishing trips, and manatees were plentiful in the Withlacoochee River which flowed adjacent to our little town.

One day Andy and I were reading together on the couch while his younger brother, Thomas, napped in his bedroom. An unfamiliar scratching and snorting sound suddenly interrupted our story. We could tell that it was coming from the yard just outside our front window. We jumped up and pressed our faces to the glass, so that we could see what was making the noise. To our surprise, we saw an armadillo digging a hole underneath the walkway leading up to our front door.

This was a golden opportunity to expand our collection of wildlife pictures, so I hurried to get my camera as Andy kept an eye on the potential highlight of our photo album. Camera retrieved, we quietly, slowly and carefully opened the front door and peeked around the corner to see if the armadillo was still there. We saw that he had walked to the end of the house, so we tiptoed across the threshold and stooped down to get the best angle we could for our photograph.

Just as I was aiming the camera, the armadillo looked up, saw us, and made a mad dash *toward* us. We had not expected or planned for this turn of events. With a sudden rush of adrenaline, I screamed, pushed Andy through the open doorway, and lunged in behind him. Was that armadillo planning an attack? It seemed so unlikely, but there was no other apparent explanation. We looked out the window, and there was the armadillo back at his freshly-dug hole. I was determined to get to the bottom of this seemingly bizarre behavior.

Fortunately, we had a two-volume set of the *National Geographic Book of Mammals*. We found our visiting armadillo in Volume 1 which contained Aardvark to Jerboa. We discovered these facts: 1) "Armadillos are well-equipped for digging. The stocky animals have short front feet with powerful, curved claws. They use these to dig underground burrows . . . ." 2) "Armadillos are timid animals. When frightened, they run for their dens. Inside their burrows they are safe." 3) "An armadillo can also protect itself by digging a new place to hide. It rapidly makes a tunnel and vanishes before a predator's eyes."[3]

Andy and I surmised that when we had initially heard the scratching and snorting of our armadillo, perhaps, because he was in unknown territory, he was digging a new place to hide. When we went outside to take his picture, our timid friend was frightened and ran for his new den (even though it was straight toward the perceived danger). He wasn't charging at us; he was simply trying to reach the safety of his new burrow.

I didn't ever get the desired photo, but I did gain a poignant insight. In Scripture, David says of God: *"You are my hiding place; you will protect me from trouble and surround me with songs of deliverance"* (Psalm 32:7). I honestly wondered at the time if God had created the armadillo with this lesson in mind.

The answer to my third question, W*here do I run in the tough times?* can be found in David's description of God: *He is our hiding place*. Just like the armadillo, when I am faced with danger or trouble, my instinct or reflex should be to immediately run toward my safe burrow. God is always there. His protection is ever available, and He Himself is my hiding place.

I don't know about you, but when I face trouble, I often start organizing or cleaning something. I think it's because I find comfort in having control over my immediate environment. I may not be able to control the troubling circumstance I'm facing, but I can certainly bring order to my desk. Some women may shop—a new dress or pair of shoes can lift the emotions and provide a pleasant, though, temporary distraction. Others eat, drink, or medicate. For some, Facebook is their diversion of choice.

God desires for us to come to the point where we recognize that He is the first place we should run when difficulty comes:

God is our refuge and strength,
A very present help in trouble,
Therefore we will not fear, though the earth should change,
And though the mountains slip into the heart of the sea;
Though its waters roar and foam,
Though the mountains quake at its swelling pride (Psalm 46:1-3).

The ultimate answer to all three of our questions is *GOD*. He is enough. And that fact, when understood and embraced, can produce great fruit in our marriages. Our husbands can't be the fulfillment of all our needs, dreams and desires. But when we quench our thirst at God's fountain, we will be strengthened, sustained, and equipped to be wives who bring blessing, stability and joy to our marriages. God can fill our hearts with His love and grant us the resplendent experience of discovering that He is enough.

Hannah Whitall Smith (1832-1911) wrote a beautiful book called *God is Enough.* Her words give voice to my prayer for you wives who have become so dear to me in the months of writing this book. My great desire for you is that God would fill your hearts and your lives with the life-giving and life-changing discovery that He is enough:

> The greatest lesson a soul has to learn is that God, and God alone, is enough for all its needs. This is the lesson that all God's dealings with us are meant to teach, and this is the crowning discovery of our entire Christian life. GOD IS ENOUGH!
>
> No soul can really be at rest until it has given up dependence on everything else and has been forced to depend on the Lord alone. As long as our expectation is from other things, nothing but disappointment awaits us. Feelings may change, doctrines and dogmas may be upset, the Christian work may come to naught, prayers may seem to lose their fervency, promises may seem to fail, everything that we have believed in or depended on may seem to be swept away, and only God is left—just God, the bare God, if I may be allowed the expression, simply and only God.
>
> If God is what He would seem to be from His revealings, if He is indeed the "God of all comfort" (2 Corinthians 1:3); if He is our Shepherd; if He is really and truly our Father; if, in short, all the many aspects He has told us of His character and His ways are actually true, then we must come to the positive conviction that He

is, in Himself alone, enough for all our needs and that we may safely rest in Him absolutely and forever. . . . When only that which cannot be shaken remains, we learn to have our expectation from Him alone.[4]

[1] Elisabeth Elliot, *A Path Through Suffering*, 87.

[2] Beth Moore, *Praying God's Word* (Nashville, TN: Broadman & Holman Publishers, 2000), 90-91.

[3] *National Geographic Book of Mammals, Vol. 1* (The National Geographic Society, Washington D.C., 1981), 63-64.

[4] Hannah Whitall Smith, *God is Enough,* (Grand Rapids, MI, Francis Asbury Press, 1986), 87.

Chapter Ten

Wise Wives Share Their Stories

Even at the beginning of my thinking and praying about this book, I wanted to include perspectives other than my own. I see things from my point of view, and my own experiences are the ones I know best. But I know many godly women, and I love to hear them teach and share, because I can benefit from the personal lessons God has taught them in the specific challenges of their marriages. So, that is the rationale for this chapter: it's an opportunity to hear from other women who have experienced God's faithfulness in the pilgrimage of marriage and are learning to love their husbands by His abundant grace.

The Wives Speak

I asked the ladies this question: **"What is one thing you didn't know before marriage that you wish you had understood?**

June Cleaver in Skinny Jeans

I grew up watching my parents set a wonderful example for me of what a godly marriage looks like in "real life." I took this example and was determined to follow it when I married my husband. However, before we got married, I never really dug into the Word to see *why* my parents did what they did, and I snagged a few outside ideas along the way. I thought I liked the idea of my husband having the final say in situations. I was sure I would agree with him, or else why would I have picked him to marry? I pictured blissful ignorance about financial matters and saying things like, "Honey, I need my money for the week." I liked the idea of my man being a spiritual leader, initiating Bible Study and family devotions. I liked the idea of being provided for, of my husband earning and handling the money while I handled the house—kind of like June Cleaver in skinny jeans with plenty of spending money.

My husband was not raised in a Christian home, and he had never had a positive male role model in his life. He was also a relatively new Christian when we got married. So here he was—a new husband who was a new Christian who had no way of knowing how to spiritually lead his new wife. We entered into marriage, and I decided that it was up to ME to be the one to coach and mold my husband into the man that God wanted him to be. It didn't occur to me that I wasn't made for this job, even though all signs pointed to the fact that I am not and never will be a man or a husband.

Like a bull in a china shop, off I went, "training and teaching" my tender-hearted husband how to love his wife like Christ loved the church. I set out to teach him how to earn my respectful and submissive attitude. I was not sensitive to his insecurity in the area of leadership. Instead of finding non-threatening ways to encourage him to lead me, I would talk to him about the things he was NOT doing as a spiritual leader. When he tried to make leadership decisions, I would be sure to tell him the better decision that God and I wanted him to make.

Oh, and also, I was a nag. I had, in all my desire to have a household modeled after Scripture, wrestled my husband's God-given role away from him. I had usurped his spiritual position in our home. I had shown him much disrespect. I had been disobedient to God's instruction to me as a wife.

God lovingly and graciously met me face to face with these grievous failures. By the conviction of the Holy Spirit, strong biblical teaching and grace-giving Titus 2 women, I started over. I had to put off these characteristics that had been defining me, these sins of self-righteousness, pride, bossiness, and dominance. I had to ask my husband for his forgiveness. I asked God to make me the godly woman and wife that He had chosen for my husband, and I had to move out of the way and quit spoiling my husband's chances to be obedient! I went into the Word, and God showed me that He made me to be my husband's help-mate. As his wife, I needed to build him up, lift him up, take burdens from him, serve him, and encourage him.

I was not made to do my husband's job and fulfill his responsibilities. That is why God gave instructions to the husband and then separate and different instructions to the wife. We have different JOBS! Respect and submission blew into our house like fresh air. I never would have thought it would be so much easier to submit to my husband than it was to try to "lead."

God has been and is still faithful in so many ways. He was faithful to undo in my husband the wrong work that I had begun. He has raised my husband up to be a strong leader, and I love it! It is an honor and privilege to watch GOD shape him to be who GOD created him to be. He has shown me the blessing of having a submissive heart and attitude. He has created a rhythm in our home that is not chaotic and loud, but one that hums along. We are far from perfect, so this hum is punctuated with the occasional clang of sinfulness. We still trip over our egos and let ourselves get in the way, but it's becoming more natural for us to grow in the direction God means for our marriage to grow. Praise God for His faithfulness! (Age 36, married 9 years)

My Husband is Not a Woman

What I most wish I had known before marriage is that my husband is not a woman! Due to the obvious, I should have known that, but I really didn't know what it meant that my husband was male. He and I were best friends. We would talk far into the night. I felt like I could tell him anything. I truly felt as if I'd found the other half of myself. And I had—it's just that my other half was completely and utterly *male*.

It's interesting to note Jesus' answer in Matthew 19 when the Pharisees were testing Him with questions regarding divorce. Jesus said, "Have you never read that He Who made them from the beginning *made them male and female,* and said, '*For this reason* a man shall leave his father and mother and shall be united to his wife, and the two shall become one flesh?'" (italics mine).

The very reason we get married in the first place is that God made us different—both in His image, but male and female. It has taken me 26 years of marriage to begin to understand this. Perhaps I'm just slow. Perhaps it's because I grew up in a culture determined to erase all differences between the sexes. Whatever the reason, that one lack of understanding has caused me much trouble in my marriage.

Several years ago, the Lord graciously allowed me to read a book called *Love and Respect*, by Dr. Emerson Eggerichs. In that book, Dr. Eggerichs talks about the Lord's command in Ephesians 5:33 for husbands to love their wives and wives to respect their husbands. He then goes on to relate that God has made us male and female, and because of that we each have different needs, desires, and ways of relating.

For women, our mother tongue is love. We're pretty good at showing love—or so we think. For men, it's all about respect. Then we marry. We show love, love, love, and that is what we want to receive. The catch is that we want to receive love our way. Our husbands believe they are showing us love as they provide for us by working long hours, caution us, tell us how to solve our problems, ask us to go motorcycle riding or sitting in a deer stand with them—and topping it all off with sex.

We become perplexed. This is not how **we** would show love. We would be home in time for dinner every night, bringing flowers and chocolate. We would never try to fix problems. We would just listen with great empathy. We would fix the leaky faucet or the broken toilet if we wanted to show love. We would suggest an activity where we could do something meaningful—like talk. We would talk while holding hands strolling through someplace beautiful—and then when the time and the mood and the circumstances were all just right and we felt physically attractive and everything smelled good and there were no dirty clothes on the floor, we'd make love.

That is how it is supposed to go. Unfortunately, because I didn't understand that God created my husband male, it usually went more like this: After working late, my husband would come home tired to a tired wife who had been dreaming of a bigger house, perhaps one that had a playroom to confine the children's toys. He would sense something was wrong and ask. I would tell him. I would tell him everything. He would go into "fix-it mode" and tell me exactly what to do. (They pay him to do this at work).

My irritation would grow. Frustrated, he would suggest we go watch a war movie or go out in the yard and weed. When he noticed that these suggestions did not excite me, he would try one last, desperate attempt to connect. He would begin to nuzzle my neck and suggest we go upstairs. I would become disgusted, because he just didn't get it. We'd both retreat nursing our disappointment. Two people who loved each other without a clue. He felt completely disrespected. I felt totally unloved.

When I began to understand that God had made my husband male, I truly began to love him. In fact, I don't think I ever truly did love him until I accepted that God had created him male, and that I was to respect him—not because he was always right, but because God commanded it.

There are days when I balk at respect and submission—days where I feel misunderstood and unloved. There are days where I *know* I'm right about something, and I get angry at God for not straightening out my husband. Then I remember the day I cried out to God. I asked Him why He wasn't speaking to my husband regarding a particular issue, and the Lord replied, "I AM speaking to him, but you are being so loud, he can't hear Me." So, I'm learning what it really means to be still and know that HE is God. In respecting and submitting to my husband, I am really respecting and submitting to God. (Age 51, married 26 years)

Gospel-Saturated Marriage

The first 15 years of my marriage were marked by church attendance, Bible studies and a sincere desire to build a Christian marriage. Yet, I would not call either my husband or myself "gospel-informed." I naively limited the gospel to my initial salvation (the gospel was the "good news" that Jesus died to save me from my sins and to secure for me a place in heaven). But I failed to see a connection between the gospel and my marriage. However, over the years the Holy Spirit has revealed that the gospel is like a packet of dye which, when added to a vat of garments, colors everything that it touches, including marriage.

As an "older woman," my desire is that young wives experience the power of the gospel in their marriages. Here are two gospel facts which I like to share with them:

1. I am a sinner married to a sinner. Both of us are in desperate need of the Savior's rescue. Knowing this will prevent me from focusing on my spouse's flaws, and rather, help me to admit my own sins. It keeps me from becoming haughty, self-righteous and critical as I understand how my sins alone warranted the death of the beautiful Son of God. Reminding myself of the sinfulness of my own sins enables me to show grace to my husband and to keep my heart sweet toward him.

   Here's how this recognition that I AM A SINNER filtered down into my daily life. For 32 years, my husband would bring the morning newspaper inside and then toss the plastic sleeve onto the kitchen counter. And for 32 years, I had picked it up and tossed it into the trash can; an act that took me all of three seconds. However, a few years ago, I began feeling an irritation because of his insensitivity in "making me" pick up the sleeve after him. So, as I focused on him and his wrongdoing, I saw him as the offender, the ungrateful husband who took advantage of my goodness (for three seconds every day!). Fortunately, the gospel truth that I, too, am a sinner came to my rescue, as I was able to detect an equally offensive resentment, self-righteousness and critical heart in me! As I repented of my own sins and received God's grace, I could extend that same grace to my husband. I am so glad that I discovered how practical the gospel is in marriage.

2. The second gospel fact I like to share is that the gospel is the "power of God." As I am gospel-saturated, its power changes me, my desires, my behavior, and my words. The gospel "centers" me to prevent self from dominating me. How I wish I had known the gospel resource available to me during those early years of marriage!

In my new desire to become gospel-saturated, I am experiencing a power beyond my own to love more completely, to forgive more deeply, to serve more willingly, and to honor more graciously. (Age 63, married 36 years)

Unfulfilled Expectations

As a little girl, I loved fairy tales—especially the ones where the damsel and the prince live "happily ever after." You see, I grew up in a home where there was anything but "happily ever after."

Dysfunctional hardly begins to describe the family in which I grew up. I longed for my life and my future marriage to be different from that of my parents. As I grew into my late teens, I still hoped that life would offer something to me that resembled a fairy tale. So, when I met my future husband (whom I believed came from a normal family), my hopes began to soar. I met him just two weeks before the end of my junior year of high school. He was looking forward to his graduation in just two weeks.

My dad made it clear that there would be no wedding until I had completed my college education. I immediately became focused, so that I could graduate in 3½ years. The plan worked: we graduated one day, and our wedding was the next day.

It turned out that neither my husband nor I had grown up in homes with godly role models. We learned quickly that dysfunction only produces more dysfunction. Even in our dating relationship, I had regarded my future husband as my redemption from the past and as my savior for the present. No one can live up to that high standard and my husband was no exception. Early in our marriage, we both realized we were experiencing unfulfilled expectations. We struggled to "get it right" for many years.

(Briefly, let me say that a wife should never put her husband on a pedestal. He will have nowhere to go but to fall off! Of course, when my prince began to act like himself—a man—I was very disappointed. Doing everything in my power to make him who I wanted him to be just about did us both in! My fantasy had dissolved before my eyes, and reality had set in. Now what was I to do? He was human!)

By our mid-thirties, Christ began to make Himself known in both of our lives. We knew all along that we were both Christians, but we didn't know how to live that out in our marriage. We both recommitted our lives to Christ and began a new journey with Him as our focus and as the head of our family.

Hard times didn't stop! It seemed as we grew older and put our trust more fully in Christ that the hard times actually intensified. Perhaps you might recognize some of our challenges: one very difficult set of in-laws (mine, of course), children making bad choices, a prodigal child, my husband's periodic criticism, my periodic nagging, health issues, financial insecurities, and even my complete discontentment. Quite frankly, I sometimes just wanted to run away.

So, even though we were both Christians, we realized that we had both married sinners! There really is no choice about that; there is no one else out there but sinners! BUT, God is faithful and completely trustworthy! We will be celebrating our 45th anniversary in a couple of months. Add to that the 4½ years we dated, and it's almost 50 years together. Such a loooooong time!

What we have learned through all our years together is that we cannot change anyone but ourselves. We cannot even do that alone; real change is only possible through God's transforming power at work in our minds and our attitudes. We also learned that when God changes us, He also works in those around us! This was such a turning point in our marriage.

God guides and directs our paths by His loving, firm discipline (unpleasant at times), and by his abundant mercy and grace. Proverbs 3:5-6 says, *"Trust in the Lord with all thine heart, lean not on thine own understanding* (so hard to do)*, in all thy ways acknowledge Him, and He will direct thy path."*

God has hammered this out in our marriage over and over. He was faithful, He is faithful, and He will be faithful. He sent His Son as my Savior. And He gave my husband to me as a gift for all my days.

Marriage is hard. It takes all three—Christ, husband, wife—to make it work. I now know life is no fairy tale. My greatest desire is that my life and my marriage bring glory to Him who sits on the throne. I will forever be His grateful daughter. (Age 66, married 45 years)

A Work in Progress

Eight years ago, I was preparing for my upcoming wedding and marriage. As a part of our premarital counseling, my fiancé and I were asked to rate on a scale of 1-10 how happy our parents were in their marriages. Both of us could very easily say that we would rate our parents very high on this scale—a 9 or 10. We both came from stable families where Christian values and morals were taught and modeled. Our parents were happily married and raised us in Christ-centered homes. We completed all the surveys, answered all the questions, and talked about our opinions on everything from who would do the dishes, to how many kids we would have, to managing our finances, to disciplining our children. We had it all covered. Right??

Now, seven years later, I realize that discussing life issues ahead of time and coming from a Christian heritage don't necessarily mean that marriage is going to be smooth sailing. After all, it is a lot easier to handle something in a certain way when it is a hypothetical situation than when the reality of something is hitting me right in the face. When the budget actually gets tight, when the toddler is throwing an actual tantrum, when day-to-day irritations begin to weigh me down—it is then that I find that although my standards have not changed, my stamina to follow through might not be as strong as I had thought. It's not that I have changed my thinking—it's just that it is a little harder than I realized to follow through.

For young people in my generation, it seems very difficult not to get caught up in the sin of comparison. Everywhere we turn, there is something thrown in our faces that says, "You're not good enough." "She's a better wife." "Look how her husband serves her." "Her husband adores her." We see it on Facebook. We see it on blogs. We see it on Twitter. But it isn't always real. After all, who would sit down at their computer and write a blog about the hurtful things her husband said or give the details of a terrible argument. Things just aren't always as they seem.

When we participate in the sin of comparison, we forget the truth of the way we were created. All different. Every one of us. When we fall in the trap of comparing our husbands to others, we forget that they bring their own strengths to the table. The enemy is always on the prowl, and if we haven't found a fault in our husbands on our own, Satan will be happy to lead us to several we haven't even noticed yet.

As young girls and women, we think that if we could just find our Prince Charming, he would rescue us from loneliness and be our constant companion. We would never suffer again from self-doubt, because he would always be there to tell us how beautiful, smart and funny we are. However, it only takes a few years into marriage before we find out that our husbands aren't satisfying all our needs. But there is a reason for that—they aren't supposed to. We are trying to put our husbands in a God-shaped hole. They are not supposed to fit.

My husband has a lot of responsibilities as a Christian husband and father. But satisfying all my needs is not on the to-do list that God has given him. My marriage is still a "work in progress," but remembering that the only place I can truly be satisfied is in the grip of my Savior's hand has helped me to balance the expectations that I place on the shoulders of my husband. (Age 29, married 7 years)

God's Design for Marriage

When I walked down the aisle on my wedding day, my head was filled with the hopes and dreams of my "happily ever after" and the love of my "prince charming." The thought of conflicts, struggles, hardships, and heartaches was not even a blip on my radar. I thought that working hard together, going to church, and exercising self-control would make a successful, blissful marriage. In my thinking, it was all about performance. We were at the center of my life, and everything revolved around us. We would make it work and have exactly what each of us desired from this union. I did not realize that God's purpose for marriage was altogether different.

When I was in the ninth grade, my father passed away unexpectedly. Not having a father during my high school and college years affected what I thought about marriage and set me on a course of "I can do it myself." I had Plan A, Plan B, and even in some instances Plan C. Everything was covered. I thought that I could make my marriage work without help. I would do whatever was needed.

My belief was that if I could be pretty enough and efficient enough, if I could act with a servant's heart (with my teeth clenched and my heart thoroughly disguised), if I could spend one more sleepless night beside my sick child's bed, if I could scrimp on groceries so that there would be money for my husband's golf clubs, then surely the result would be praise and positive reciprocation from my husband. However, I soon learned that this manipulation did not work.

It wasn't long before I realized that my ideas, thoughts, and ways of doing things were not necessarily compatible with those of my husband. My prince charming had become a fallible flesh-and-blood person. I was also not the princess I had daydreamed of being, nor was I as important to my husband as I thought I should be. I was a human being with an emptiness in my heart which my spouse could not fill.

In the fourth year of my marriage, I remember sitting in the balcony of a small Baptist church hoping that no one could see me crying. The realization that I alone could not create a happy marriage was an unbearable weight and heartbreak. I was a failure.

It was then that I began to understand that I needed Jesus and His grace to enable and sustain me. This began my search to discover what God's intentions were for my life and my marriage. I had to look at my controlling heart, at my selfish agenda, at what Christ's death on the cross really meant. I began to grasp the true purpose of marriage and how much I needed to depend on Him. I began to realize that marriage was about God's work in me—to change me and to sanctify me. I learned and am learning that marriage is much more about my relationship with God than it is about my relationship with my husband. God's glory and our joy are intertwined. (Age 67, married 37 years)

Two Good Forgivers

No one told me that marriages that last are made up of two good forgivers! Before I married, I never thought that there would be anything substantial to forgive! We were in love, we had a detailed "plan," a deep commitment, and similar goals. Wasn't that enough? My future husband was so loyal and honorable. How would he ever do anything for which he would need to be forgiven?

Sure, we had different personalities; we give new meaning to the words "extrovert" and "introvert"! We came from polar opposite family dynamics. He is a "big picture" guy, and I am a detail manager. I thought that sports were something occasionally on television, and he thought that the seasons of the year were defined by sports!

I can't go to sleep "at odds" with anyone (it must be addressed now!), and he likes to mull it over for a while, and then let it go. I came from a very long line of strict disciplinarians, and his childhood was loosely monitored with few boundaries. His idea of financial planning was a monthly budget with little flexibility and lots of cash reserves, and my idea was recording all my withdrawals and transactions (occasionally) after the fact.

So, what would there be to forgive? Why should I expect conflict and differences of opinion? Wouldn't we just stop everything and sit down and rationally come to a consensus about what we should do? Wouldn't we always clearly see what decision to make based on what was best for the other? Why would either of us have to walk away from a discussion in frustration, disappointment, or even worse, anger? With stars in our eyes and dreams in our hearts, why would either of us "hold onto" the disagreement and become bitter, resentful or withdrawn?

No one told me that there are so many opportunities in marriage where there would be a need for forgiving the one I love. No one said it would be much easier and a more natural response NOT to forgive. No one told me how to forgive or why I would need to. I don't even remember the word "forgiveness" coming up in our premarital counseling. I remember the pastor saying that we might have some "ups and downs" because of our different approaches to life. But surely our love and commitment would take care of that!

It took a little while to see that marriage was a continual series of opportunities to forgive. Forgiveness was for issues that were large and small, important and trivial, flexible and non-negotiable. It was for issues that were immediate and ongoing, for the intentional and unintentional. It took time to learn that forgiving each other for small daily things and huge bad decisions was critical for our marriage to move forward and grow as it should through the years.

Why is forgiving so important? Because Jesus commands us to forgive. He calls us to follow His example. We forgive, not because our spouse deserves it, but because we want to be transformed into a new creature in Christ. Ephesians 4:32 says, *"Be kind and compassionate to one another, forgiving each other, just as in Christ God forgave you."*

So, what is marriage? The union of two good forgivers! (Age 55, married 32 years)

The Seasons of Marriage

> *Though the fig tree does not bud and there are no grapes on the vines, though the olive crop fails and the fields produce no food, though there are no sheep in the pen and no cattle in the stalls, yet I will rejoice in the Lord* (Habakkuk 3:17).

I like sitting on my front porch in the rain. It is quiet, peaceful, relaxing. Across the pasture is a huge wall of trees displaying God's splendor, majesty, and uniqueness—each tree different, no two are the same. They dance to and fro to the music of the breeze; the birds are quiet and unseen, waiting for the rain to stop so they can come forth again to continue their singing.

One tree, however, always catches my eye. It is different. It doesn't sway in the wind like the others, but stands firm and rigid, as though it were tired and worn out. It no longer wears leaves or houses birds. Most would say it is dead and should be cut down.

I got married at age 20. My expectations for married life were nothing less than blissful love and happiness. I did not come to this conclusion by the example I grew up with. In fact, quite the opposite was true. My dad was an alcoholic who committed suicide when I was ten. At age thirteen, I was placed in a boarding school, never again to live at home. Consequently, I dreamed of a *happy* home, and I felt sure of the future . . . after all, I had married a wonderful man (I still believe he's a wonderful man, just in case you're wondering). This *happiness* was a noble goal, but in retrospect, it was a worldly happiness that I was seeking. I wanted to have the perfect house, family and love . . . the kind of love I experienced when I was first married . . . that would last "happily ever after."

Because my expectation was for a lasting happiness, I was unprepared for the one constant and inevitable event in every marriage—change. When I say I was unprepared for change, I'm not talking about the good changes like kids, job promotions, moves, grandkids, etc. I'm talking about the seasons of marriage that force our dependence on God, not on the world. As I look back over the 43 years my husband and I have been married, not all the changes have been good ones, but all were *necessary.* Like the seasons, each one brought a different kind of change, a lesson to be learned and a promise to hold on to. As Solomon writes, *"There is a time for everything, a season for every activity under heaven"* (Ecclesiastes 3:1).

There are many seasons in a marriage, but I want to focus on one that I believe is relevant to the majority of present-day marriages, and that is the season of fall. Most people look forward to fall because of its beauty. The beautiful colors that paint the land are pleasing, just as our spouses are in the beginning of a marriage. But as time moves on, the temperatures cool. The colors fade and cease to display any beauty. Eventually the leaves fall to the ground, leaving what appears to be a lifeless tree.

Marriage can be like that. It starts out with great vibrancy and beauty, but things start to change. Dreams cease to come true. Expectations are not met. Noises, smells, habits, moods . . . you name it . . . grind on and on, day after day, until the fallen leaves are our primary focus. We begin to feel as if this season will never move on, and if it does, what will it bring?

The truth is, we can't have fall until summer has passed. The beauty and new life of spring can't come until winter has passed. The cycles of seasons created by God are necessary in nature. They are also necessary in marriages. These cycles can be hard—very hard. In my marriage, I had to learn to stop dwelling on the season, and start to focus more on what God was trying to teach me. Psalm 1:2-3 speaks of this: *". . . but his delight is in the law of the Lord, and on His law he meditates day and night. He is like a tree planted by streams of water which yields its fruit in its season, and its leaf does not wither. In all that he does, he prospers."*

The tall tree still stands across the pasture. I'm glad I never cut it down, because it is a constant reminder that God is still at work in my life and marriage, preparing me for a new season. The world would say that the tree is dead and should be cut down, but I know differently. Buds are forming in the darkness and at the right season, in His perfect timing, they will bring forth new life and beauty. Then as new leaves grow and become strong, that tired tree will once again dance in the breeze . . . rejoicing!

So, in the light of what I've learned over the years, when the next season comes, I will take a seat on my front porch and remember the seasons past, and how God was faithful and true to His word. I pray the same will be true for you as you trust the Lord in all the seasons of your life and marriage. (Committed to marriage for 43 years, still learning at age 64, praising the Lord for His grace and mercy)

Grace for the Journey

> *For everything there is a season, and a time for every matter under heaven: a time to be born, and a time to die; a time to plant, and a time to pluck up what is planted; a time to kill, and a time to heal; a time to break down, and a time to build up; a time to weep, and a time to laugh; a time to mourn, and a time to dance; a time to cast away stones, and a time to gather stones together; a time to embrace, and a time to refrain from embracing; a time to seek, and a time to lose; a time to keep, and a time to cast away; a time to tear, and a time to sew; a time to keep silence, and a time to speak; a time to love, and a time to hate; a time for war, and a time for peace* (Ecclesiastes 3:1-8).

Trying to write about marital advice when you find yourself in a fantastic blessed season of wedded bliss is challenging. While I type this, all seems well within my little bubble in the world. Even digging deep into my memory, those terrible years of fighting, of contemplating separation, of plotting my escape, of my utter hatred for my husband seem vague, far away and nearly unbelievable. And yet, all of that ugliness is part of my marriage history. I know it is possible for it to happen again, although I pray not.

Why do I believe this? Because I am a sinful, selfish, self-promoting human, as is my husband and everyone else around me. Once we begin to believe that we deserve more, we are doomed. Once we take the step to make life *fair*, we are doomed. Once we decide to stand up for our rights, we are doomed. We act on these impulses, rather than taking it to the Lord. We lash out with words that hurt, rather than remain silent. We act in disrespectful and dishonoring ways, rather than trust that it is His battle.

We are humans prone to acting on our feelings and emotions. Yet, we fail to recognize that the basis on which we plot our actions is likely to change within a couple of weeks, days, or even minute to minute. Life is full of these changes, these *seasons* of intense feelings of highs and lows. The key word here is *"season."* After fourteen years of marriage, I realize that I started my marriage off as a passenger on the world's tallest, fastest and steepest roller coaster. This resulted in *seasons* of complete emotional turmoil ranging from exhilaration to extreme nausea. The negative emotions and wild swings outweighed the positive ones. Somehow, by the grace of God and strong Christian mentors, I learned how to exit that disastrous ride.

The first year of my marriage was the worst year of my life. My battles with my husband began even before we were married and continued to build throughout the first months of our wedded life. They culminated in arguments about how we would celebrate Christmas. Our very heated discussions lasted at least a month before Christmas and then well into the New Year.

Our ideas about how to spend time and money during the holidays was representative of every conflict we had—always about time and money. It was a battle of the wills—two independent, controlling, extremely Type-A people trying to co-exist. The hateful fighting only intensified after our first Christmas, and by February, I was planning how to leave my husband. We had been married for 5 months. I was defeated and crushed. I remember thinking that I could never really love my husband again after the things we had said and done. I believed my marriage was all one big, horrible mistake.

Back in those early dark days of my marriage, a dear Christian sister shed some light on the situation. She implored me to stick it out, to remember my commitment, to give it more time. It was hard for me to believe her, because I felt as if my utter disdain for this person I was living with could never change. Yet, I stayed. I stayed by the grace and mercy of God.

Slowly, time became my friend. The years have passed; the seasons have changed: seasons that have included intense arguing and soul-shattering pain; seasons of laughter and the thrill at the birth of our children; seasons of hurt and withdrawal; seasons of joy and contentment; seasons of success and failure. There were times during which we were clearly hearing the Lord and letting Him guide us, and times where we tried to take the reins and control our destiny.

As I type this, there are several marriages around me that are crumbling. Spouses are planning their own escapes—not because of adultery or abuse, but because they are fed-up, hurt, angry, irritated, done with trying. I honestly want to scream at them, "Give it another six months, or even a year! It will all change!" Even now, when I find myself at the top of the hill, bottoming out, or pulling into the platform, I know that something else is around the bend—it is all *seasonal!*

I have a sticker on my bathroom mirror that reminds me daily, "This too will pass away, but the love of Christ will forever stay." It is a perfect reminder that our journey on this earth is full of challenges and changes. So please remember, do your best to stay on the kiddie coaster and to remember that even when your stomach feels like it has fallen to your feet, it is just a season. (Age 40, married 14 years)

Epilogue

One Final Thought: A Costly Love

For the love of Christ controls us, having concluded this, that One died for all, therefore all died; and He died for all, that they who live should no longer live for themselves, but for Him Who died and rose again on their behalf. 2 Corinthians 5:14-15

The love of Christ that God makes available *to* us and *through* us is costly: it requires two deaths. The first death occurred almost 2000 years ago. Christ's substitutionary death on the cross paid the penalty for our sin, so that we might be forgiven and live for eternity with God in Heaven. Christ's death paved the way for a second necessary death: our death to self.

This death to self is possible because of our salvation. With our new life comes a new power to live and love in God's way. Jesus made a promise to His disciples that when He departed, He would ask the Father to *"give you another Helper, that He may be with you forever; that is the Spirit of truth, whom the world cannot receive, because it does not behold Him or know Him, but you know Him because He abides with you, and will be in you"* (John 14:16-17). The Holy Spirit is our Helper . . . forever.

Paul confirms this truth in Romans 5:5: *". . . the love of God has been poured out within our hearts through the Holy Spirit who was given to us."* The "ingredients" (the indwelling presence of the Holy Spirit and the grace of God) are in place to make it possible for us to love as Christ loved. But, as I mentioned earlier, it requires a second death.

In John 12:24-25, Jesus describes this necessary death: *"Truly, truly, I say to you, unless a grain of wheat falls into the earth and dies, it remains by itself alone; but if it dies, it bears much fruit. He who loves his life loses it; and he who hates his life in this world shall keep it to life eternal."* Christ's death on the cross (which provided salvation) was a one-time historical event. Our death to self is a present, repeatable, and continuous process. It's a choice made possible by the power of God's Spirit who lives in us, and by God's grace which He offers freely to all of His children.

From Infancy to Adulthood

There's a picture in my memory of my middle son sitting solemnly on our couch with a cardboard badge pinned to his striped shirt. Printed on the badge is the statement: "I'm two today." I vividly remember a feeling of aching wistfulness as I contemplated the speed with which my little boys were growing up.

Though I had moments of melancholy, I took great delight in each stage of my sons' development. I loved to watch them as they found their feet for the first time, as they toddled around the room and plopped down heavily on their diapered bottoms, as they discovered that words could get them what they wanted, and as they learned to build precarious towers with their blocks. I would have been dismayed and frightened by any perceived delay in their anticipated growth.

The stages of growth that we expect in our children's development from infancy to childhood, and from adolescence to adulthood, are a visible and physical representation of the growth that we should expect to see in a Christian's spiritual life. Salvation gives us new life—eternal life. Sanctification (the process of Christian growth and transformation) is our development from spiritual infancy to an ever-increasing spiritual maturity and Christlikeness. This process, which involves a daily dying to self, continues until our physical death.

The process of sanctification is inextricably linked to marriage. God desires to use our marriages in this process of change and maturity. Just as a two-year old rebels against having to learn to share, a husband and wife rebel against having to give up their selfish ways as they learn to live together in marriage. Parents will spend many years training and disciplining their children to teach them this important lesson—it's a hard one to learn. And it's not any easier when you're learning it in the context of marriage.

As wives, we often "dig in our heels" in marriage and demand that our needs be met in our way and in our timing. We want things to be done according to our particular likes and dislikes. When this doesn't happen, the tantrums taking place in our hearts may be invisible to those around us (or very visible), but they're always apparent to God, and He is going to use the many years of our marriages to teach us to love, to serve, to forgive, to respect, to share, and ultimately to die to self.

This dying-to-self business is what makes marriage so hard. It is costly and painful. But it drives us to the cross of Christ, and that is God's intention. When we honestly recognize and confess our sin (e.g., anger, selfishness, unforgiveness, impatience, bitterness, self-pity, comparing, disrespect, self-righteousness), then there is help and hope for our predicament. The Holy Spirit is faithful to speak to our hearts about our sin. He gives us a sense of unrest and conviction. Our job is to listen to Him and to respond to Him.

It is in responding to the Holy Spirit that we are taken to the cross. God is faithful to forgive us based on the death of Christ. The payment that took place for our sin is certain. God doesn't forgive us based on anything that we feel or do. It is based completely on the cross of Christ. And when we repent and receive His forgiveness, He promises us cleansing and peace.

It's at this point that God's grace and His Spirit make it possible for us to choose to love. With a cleansed heart, we can choose to love by God's grace. Again, this love is not innate—it is God's love, and He can grant it to us, so that we are enabled to offer it to our husbands in our actions, words, and attitudes.

I want to emphasize again that this process is a true spiritual transformation. Only God can change a heart. His inexpressible power brought a universe into existence, raised our Savior from the dead, and brought salvation to thousands at Pentecost. God in the person of the Holy Spirit indwells every believer and grants us access to this life-changing and heart-transforming power. It is a life-depleting and heart-breaking tragedy to relinquish this power by a refusal to humble ourselves in our marriages: to demand our own way; to refuse to forgive or respect; to hold onto our expectations; to judge and compare.

Marriage is hard. It pushes us to the cross. It's there that we find hope, motivation and power to learn how to do the challenging job of being a godly wife. I've been at it for over 29 years, and I'm not sure that it will ever be an easy or trouble-free endeavor. But it can become the most fulfilling vocation you've ever had as you submit to God's purposes for marriage, to be a woman who is becoming increasingly conformed to the image of Christ, and to build, by God's grace, a marriage that ever more brings glory to Him.

I love the words of this old hymn that I regularly sang in church as a young girl. It was written by Elvina M. Hall in 1865. The title expresses the greatest hope that this life holds—the hope that ultimately gives purpose, power and promise to our marriages:

Jesus Paid It All

I hear the Savior say,
"Thy strength indeed is small!
Child of weakness, watch and pray,
Find in Me thine all in all."

Lord, now indeed I find
Thy power, and Thine alone,
Can change the leper's spots
And melt this heart of stone.

For nothing good have I
Whereby Thy grace to claim—
I'll wash my garments white
In the blood of Calvary's Lamb.

Jesus paid it all,
All to Him I owe;
Sin had left a crimson stain—
He washed it white as snow.

May your hope be found in that costly love that went to the cross for you, so that you may be a willing vessel through which Christ's love will be made manifest in your marriage! Amen.

Discussion Questions

Chapter 1: My Love is Not Enough

1. How would you answer Susan's question to the newlyweds at the rehearsal dinner: "What did you experience in the early years of your marriage that you were not expecting or were unprepared for?

2. Did you have any "warning" prior to your wedding that marriage could be so hard?

3. How did you define "love" before your marriage? Did you think that it would be so tough?

4. How do you think current cultural trends deceive young women about the true nature of love and marriage?

5. Discuss the following false definitions of love: sexual attraction; infatuation; "need"-satisfaction. How do they undermine marriage?

6. Describe a "tremendous trifle" you have encountered in your marriage. How can you respond to your husband with biblical love regarding your tremendous trifle? Does love mean that you always overlook every tremendous trifle?

7. Which expression of love in 1 Corinthians 3:4-7 is most difficult for you? How does this chapter help us to understand that love is not primarily a feeling?

8. What is one specific application you can make this week to actively love your husband?

9. Write a prayer to God expressing your commitment to purposefully love your husband this week. Ask God for His grace to help you follow through with your plan. (The Holy Spirit will be faithful to remind you and to supply creativity. Keep your heart attuned to His prompting and obey by the strength that He supplies.)

Chapter 2: The Depth of My Sin

1. What is the first sin you remember committing? How did you feel afterwards?

2. When did you first become aware that you are a sinner?

3. What is the difference between sins of commission and sins of omission? Why are we often unaware of our sins of omission?

4. What does Psalm 51:5 mean when it says, *"I was sinful at birth"*?

5. What is the difference between **feeling** guilty and **being** guilty? Which one is the bigger problem for us?

6. Talk about the gift that God has given to women of relational warmth and responsiveness. What is the temptation that corresponds to this gift?

7. Share an example of a difference in the way you and your husband were raised. How has that been a source of conflict or misunderstanding in your marriage? Have you found a solution or compromise to solve this conflict?

8. Discuss Gary Thomas' quote on p. 19. What is the lesson of the toothpaste tube?

9. Are you more often a "blamer" or an "avoider" when you are squeezed? What is the biblical alternative to blaming and avoiding?

10. What is the connection between understanding the depth of my sin and my ability to "love much"?

11. What is your personal application from Chapter 2?

Chapter 3: The Magnitude of God's Grace, Part One

1. Share the story of your salvation experience.

2. Did you know in your early Christian life that you were supposed to be growing spiritually? When did you become aware of that truth?

3. What is grace? Why is God's grace essential for building a marriage that glorifies God?

4. What is meant by the phrase "instruments of God's grace"?

5. What is the first instrument of God's grace discussed in Chapter 3? Why is it a necessary component of a successful marriage?

6. Share an experience when God spoke personally to your heart through a passage of Scripture.

7. Why is it so difficult to be consistent in reading God's Word?

8. Share any ideas which have helped you to be more consistent in spending time with God in His Word.

9. Pray together as a group that God would help you to be creative in making time to spend with Him in His Word. Acknowledge to God your understanding of your need for the wisdom, instruction, and encouragement in His Word. Make a renewed commitment to be an active participant in this instrument of God's grace.

Chapter 4: The Magnitude of God's Grace, Part Two

1. Review together the meaning of the phrase "instruments of God's grace." What was the first instrument of grace we discussed in Chapter 3?

2. Explain how Jesus incorporated prayer as an instrument of God's grace in His earthly life. What was His instruction to the disciples in the Garden of Gethsemane?

3. What is an example of a time when you personally should pray in anticipation of a particular temptation (Example: before a stressful phone call when you know you'll need patience and wisdom)?

4. Why is it often a struggle to have a concentrated or extended time of prayer?

5. How does God use the body of Christ to strengthen our relationship to Him?

6. Explain the importance of obedience in the parable of the wise man and the foolish man. What provides us with a firm foundation for our lives and marriages?

7. How does God use suffering and trials in the lives of His children? Share an example from your own experience.

8. How is your marriage impacted when you participate in God's instruments of grace? How is your marriage impacted when God's instruments of grace are neglected?

9. Choose one of God's instruments of grace, and share a way that you will incorporate it more consistently into your life.

Chapter 5: Marriage is a Process—Love is Learned

1. Why do we sometimes experience "culture shock" in our marriages? Share an example from your first year of marriage.

2. Explain the phrase, "It's not wrong; it's just different."

3. Why does Paul say in Titus 2 that young women must be *"trained"* or *"taught"* to love their husbands?

4. What was the first thing Adam and Eve did after they sinned? Explain what happened next.

5. How does this hereditary self-orientation show up in our marriages?

6. Discuss the description of biblical love in Philippians 2:3-4. Make it practical. Give specific examples of how that would look in your marriage.

7. Discuss Gary Thomas' quote on p. 57. Talk about God's refining process in the crucible of marriage.

8. What is the role of grace in marriage? (Don't forget the importance of God's instruments of grace outlined in Chapters 3 and 4.)

9. Explain the process by which God actually transforms our hearts to make us more like Christ.

10. Pray together for God's heart transformation in your lives. Thank Him for His grace that makes it possible to change. Commit your way to Him for His glory and for His good purposes to be accomplished in your marriages.

Chapter 6: Expectations Can Be Deadly

1. What was one of your early expectations of married life (prior to being married)? How was your expectation formed? Did your husband or your marriage fulfill that expectation?

2. Explain and discuss the "expectation-experience gap."

3. What impact do "chick flicks" and social media have on your expectations for your husband and your marriage?

4. Discuss Romans 12:1-3. How can you make Paul's instruction practical in your relationship with your husband (in regard to expectations)?

5. In what way can expectations be idolatrous?

6. What are some biblical ways that a wife can fill the gap when her experiences don't live up to her expectations?

7. Discuss John Ensor's quote at the end of Chapter 6. Do you think he is overstating the problem of unmet expectations, or do you think his words are true to life?

8. What is a current expectation you have that may occupy idol status in your heart?

9. Pray this week that the Holy Spirit would reveal to you your idolatrous expectations. Confess them to God and ask for His help to cleanse your heart and to set you free. Fill the gap with renewed patience, kindness, and love for your husband.

Chapter 7: Respect is Given, Not Earned

1. In what way is respect an action? Are feelings ever a part of respect?

2. How is respect a "Golden Rule sort of behavior"?

3. Discuss the "missing piece of the puzzle" analogy.

4. What are the enemies of respect? (Don't limit your discussion to the examples given in the chapter.)

5. How is your verbal and non-verbal communication an indication of your respect or disrespect? Be specific.

6. What do tone, timing, and temper have to do with respect?

7. Which of the men's comments resonates most personally in your heart?

8. What effect does your disrespect for your husband have on your children? What does respect for your husband produce in your children?

Chapter 8: Forgiveness is a Choice, Not a Feeling

1. How does unforgiveness make a home into a prison?

2. How is God's forgiveness for us attained?

3. What is Jesus explaining about forgiveness in John 13:6-10 when he differentiates between a full "bath" and a "foot washing"?

4. Explain the difference between "reconciliation" and "restoration."

5. Discuss the three options you have when you have been offended: you can focus your time, emotions, and energy on . . .

    . . . the offender (your husband)
    . . . the offense (real or perceived)
    . . . your response

6. What does Isaiah 43:25 mean when it says that God "will not remember your sins"?

7. Read aloud the Spurgeon quote on p. 99. Spend a few minutes together in prayer thanking God for the death of Christ which paid the full penalty for your sin.

8. What is meant by an "attitude of forgiveness"?

9. How does God use the circumstances in our lives to teach us about how to have an attitude of forgiveness? Share a personal example.

Chapter 9: God is Enough

1. In what ways do wives expect their husbands to be "everything to them"?

2. How did Christ's death on the cross provide the way for a full and personal relationship with God?

3. In what ways are you tempted to find peace in your life apart from God? Be specific.

4. How do you prefer to fill your heart apart from God? Does it bring lasting relief or peace?

5. Where do you run in the tough times when you don't run to God? Share a specific experience.

6. Why do you so often look elsewhere for your peace, comfort, and security? What impact does that have in your relationship with your husband?

7. Read aloud together the passage from Psalm 139 on p. 104. Let it be a prayer of thanksgiving and praise to God for His perfect knowledge of you and His care for you.

Chapter 10: Wise Wives Share Their Stories

Epilogue: One Final Thought: A Costly Love

1. Which wife's story do you most personally relate to? Why?

2. How would you answer the question: "What is one thing you didn't know before marriage that you wish you had understood?"

3. Discuss the sentence: "The love of Christ that God makes available *to* us and *through* us is costly . . . it requires two deaths." Explain the two required deaths.

4. What is sanctification? What does it have to do with marriage?

5. What is meant by the phrase "love is a choice"? Is it possible for you to consistently choose to love? How can you do it? Why don't you do it?

6. Where can we find hope, motivation, and power to learn how to be a godly wife?

7. In the months and years to come, what are some specific ways that you can choose to love your husband? Brainstorm. Encourage your sisters.

8. Commit your way to God in prayer.